Hope: A Shield in the Economy of Borderline States

In this detailed examination of the way that borderline patients use hope as a means of preventing change and sustaining omnipotence, Anna Potamianou draws on her many years of clinical experience, as well as myth and literature, to put forward new ways of understanding narcissistic and borderline pathology.

She describes how, in normal individuals, hope functions as a link with the good object and rests on a self-image stable enough to wait for the object to reappear. However, she argues, hope often has its roots in narcissism and the development of a grandiose self which denies the link between the dependent child and the lost object. In the case of borderline and narcissistic patients it serves to prevent the disintegration of the ego during the period of waiting, but at a heavy cost. Loss is denied, change is prevented and mourning interfered with.

Showing how her ideas are linked to the theories of analysts such as Kohut, Kernberg, Winnicott and Green, she discusses what she sees as the two fundamental influences on narcissistic and borderline pathology. The first is the balance between cathexis and countercathexis, which determines the cohesiveness of the patient's identity and also governs the degree of contact with both internal and external reality. The second is the degree of instinctual fusion and diffusion between the life and death instincts, which determines the extent to which the patient's mental function is narcissistic or object related.

The stimulating and varied clinical examples used throughout this book to describe the different ways the borderline patients can use hope as a defence will be of interest to all analysts who are concerned to improve their understanding and treatment of such patients.

Anna Potamianou is a Training Analyst of the Paris Psychoanalytic Society and member of the Greek Study Group. She teaches at Pantios University, Greece, and is in private practice.

THE NEW LIBRARY OF PSYCHOANALYSIS

The New Library of Psychoananlysis was launched in 1987 in association with the Institute of Psycho-Analysis, London. Its purpose is to facilitate a greater and more widespread appreciation of what psychoanalysis is really about and to provide a forum for increasing mutual understanding between psychoanalysts and those working in other disciplines such as history, linguistics, literature, medicine, philosophy, psychology and the social sciences. It is intended that the titles selected for publication in the series should deepen and develop psychoanalytic thinking and technique, contribute to psychoanalysis from outside, or contribute to other disciplines from a psychoanalytical perspective.

The Institute, together with the British Psycho-Analytic Society, runs a low-fee psychoanalytic clinic, organizes lectures and scientific events concerned with psychoanalysis, publishes the *International Journal of Psycho-Analysis* (which now incorporates the *International Review of Psycho-Analysis*), and runs the only training course in the UK in psychoanalysis leading to membership of the International Psychoanalytical Association – the body which preserves internationally agreed standards of training, of professional entry and of professional ethics and practice for psychoanalysis as initiated and developed by Sigmund Freud. Distinguished members of the Institute have included Michael Balint, Wilfred Bion, Ronald Fairbairn, Anna Freud, Ernest Jones, Melanie Klein, John Rickman and Donald Winnicott.

Volumes 1–11 in the series have been prepared under the general editorship of David Tuckett, with Ronald Britton and Eglé Laufer as associate editors. Subsequent volumes are under the general editorship of Elizabeth Bott Spillius, with, from Volume 17, Donald Campbell, Michael Parsons, Rosine Jozef Perelberg and David Taylor as associate editors.

ALSO IN THIS SERIES

NEW LIBRARY OF PSYCHOANALYSIS
26

General Editor: Elizabeth Bott Spillius

Hope:
A Shield in the Economy
of Borderline States

Anna Potamianou

London and New York

First published 1997
by Routledge
11 New Fetter Lane, London EC4P 4EE
Simultaneously published in the USA and Canada
by Routledge
29 West 35th Street, New York, NY 10001

Routledge is an International Thomson Publishing Company

© 1997 Anna Potamianou
Typeset in Bembo by LaserScript Ltd, Mitcham
Printed and bound in Great Britain by
Clays Ltd, St Ives PLC

British Library Cataloguing in Publication Data
A catalogue record for this book is available from the British Library

Library of Congress Cataloging in Publication Data
Potamianou, Anna.
[Un Bouclier dans l'économie des états limites. French]
Hope: A shield in the economy of borderline states/by Anna Potamianou;
translated by Philip Slotkin.
p. cm. – (New library of psychoanalysis; 26)
Includes bibliographical references and index.
1. Borderline personality disorders.   2. Hope.   3. Other relations (Psychoanalysis)
4. Defense mechanisms (Psychology)   I. Title.   II. Series.
RC569.5.B67P68 1996
616.85'852–dc20   95–50977
CIP
ISBN 0–415–12176–0 (hbk)
ISBN 0–415–12177–9 (pbk)

Contents

Introduction

ἐάν μή ἔλπηται
ἀνέλπιστον οὐκ ἐξεὑρήσει
ἀνεξερεύνητον ἐόν καί ἄπορον

(Heraclitus)[1]

Hope in borderline states

The place of hope in the life and analysis of certain patients fixated on waiting for a future that is always 'to come', in which their wish for erotic plenitude or for strength through achievements would be fulfilled, led me to reflect on the dynamics and economy of this cathexis in these patients' minds.

In such patients, narcissistic vulnerability is coupled with grandiose ideals and the possibility of any genuine elaborative work is blocked by omnipotent fantasies. Narcissistic pathology is not accompanied in these patients by serious ego disorganization, but different degrees of weakness are observable in their ego structuring, and an underlying borderline organization may be discerned.

In previous publications (A. Potamianou, 1988 and 1990), I discussed analysands who sometimes find it very hard to function mentally. This is due not so much to a prohibition on the pleasure of functioning as to a difficulty in making use, in the analytic context, of the interplay of two processes of free association – the analysand's and the analyst's – for the purpose of an emotional experience of shared creative searching. These patients can maintain their neurotic defences as long as the disappointments of daily life or the frustrations inherent in the analytic situation do not activate their susceptibility to severe regressions and their tendency to decathect external and internal reality. I concentrated in those earlier

1

contributions on certain types of resistance, and in particular the so-called 'negative therapeutic reaction', which, I postulated, in such cases assumed particular forms not only connected with the punitive superego or with the ego's striving for punishment.

In this book I shall attempt to demonstrate the dynamic and economic value of another form of resistance, in which a stubborn hope becomes, at one and the same time, the guarantor of distressed narcissism and the shield of masochism: for and against life. Whereas hope is usually regarded as an affect that promotes development and change, here it is in the service of a series of fixations which transform its aims.

Different authors' views on the problem of borderline states

The narcissistic vulnerability responsible for profound regressive move-ments reflected in phases of over-precarious cathexis of external or internal reality, or both, sometimes extending to the point of complete decathexis, is observed in our clinical work when the structuring of conflicts and defences, as well as the transference constellation, indicate that certain forms of organization of narcissistic disorders hold sway. These situations have given rise to controversy among psychoanalysts on the importance of the distinction between narcissistic personalities and so-called borderline states. These discussions were inspired by positions such as that of H. Kohut (1966, 1971), who emphasized the need to differentiate between the pathology of narcissistic structures and borderline pathology, the relevant criterion being the sense of continuity of the self, which is more fragile in borderline patients. In simple narcissistic disorders, cohesion of the self is more secure, even if it at times appears threatened. Narcissistic deficiencies are therefore less severe here.

Conversely, O. Kernberg (1967) draws attention to the very wide spectrum of disorders involving borderline organization and notes the polymorphism of symptoms and the diversity of their configurations, which extend from narcissistic insufficiencies within a seemingly neurotic context to extreme forms of narcissistic pathology. Kernberg wrote in 1975[2] that patients suffering from borderline personality organization may present themselves with what superficially appear to be typical neurotic symptoms. The ultimate mark of the borderline personality organization is the combination of these symptoms with a structural pathology of the ego characterized by the predominance of primitive defence mechanisms (such as splitting, disavowal, primitive idealization, projective identification, omnipotence, etc.), lack of anxiety tolerance, lack of impulse control and lack of developed sublimatory channels (pp. 22–23). Kernberg considers that a degree of non-differentiation between the images of self and object and the concomitant blurring of ego boundaries are characteristic aspects of borderline pathology, resulting from disturbances of object internalization.

Other authors, such as G. Adler (1985), have tried to describe a form of organization whereby the neuroses on the one hand can be clearly distinguished from the psychoses on the other. Adler (p. 86) recommends the idea of a continuum in the conceptualization of narcissistic disorders and of the borderline organization.

In the view of J. Bergeret (1974), borderline cases cannot be characterized as 'structures', because what they lack is precisely a stable organization. In his opinion, they in fact involve often long-lasting modifications which sometimes even persist throughout life.[3] He considers (1986, p. 162) that depressive tendencies which cannot be deemed merely temporary episodes that occur during a process of structural evolution, whether neurotic or psychotic, may frequently be the only manifestations of pathology in a borderline type of mental organization – i.e., of an unstable and fragile, albeit sometimes very durable, organization. In his view, these are cases where structural development has been blocked.

D. Winnicott[4] held that these subjects, while having a psychotic nucleus, possess enough of a neurotic organization for psychotic anxiety to be contained, whereas W. Bion (1957) invoked the concepts of psychotic and non-psychotic parts of the personality.

A. Green (1983, p. 163) suggested that narcissistic and borderline patients should be included in the class of pathologies involving problems with the organization of boundaries, both internal and external; he noted that object-related drives are implicated more in classical borderline patients than in narcissistic organizations.[5] This position in my view has the merit of raising two fundamental questions:

1 that of cathexes and countercathexes. This is surely one of the most fundamental issues, as cohesion of identity and contact with internal and external reality depend on it;
2 that of the main trends of fusion and defusion of drives, which are the basis of the different modalities of psychic functioning, both narcissistic and object-related.

I have chosen in this book to concentrate on these two questions, because I believe that in the relevant patients the problem of cathexes is crucial, in both quantitative and qualitative terms, as is the issue of the fusion and defusion of drives. In my opinion, these are therefore the levels on which many questions still remain to be investigated in present-day psychoanalytic thinking.[6]

I have approached these problems as follows. In the first part of the book, I present some general ideas and related clinical configurations. The second part concentrates on the course of a binding cathexis, hope. In the borderline economy, this cathexis seems to be the result of an image of self stable enough to sustain waiting for a good object 'to come'. However, this waiting is rooted in the experience of a grandiose self, whose productions make themselves felt on the level of the dynamic and economic functioning of hope in the organization of narcissism.

Hope here proves to be stubborn in the extreme, taking the place of lost objects, so as to maintain unity in a psychic organization that would otherwise be potentially at the mercy of an as it were hurting narcissism. As an ultimate internal possession of the ego, hope here also guarantees lack of change, lack of mourning, and the least expenditure of energy.

It should be noted that the pathology of these cases may manifest itself in extreme forms only in the process of treatment, because the psychic organization it implies is often masked by combination with neurotic symptoms which persist as long as external or psychic reality is not excessively disappointing. But analysts today are prepared to acknowledge that other models have developed since those of neurosis and dreams on which the Freudian universe was originally based. These models correspond to the psychic functioning of patients who are to a greater or lesser extent unable to rediscover, reconstruct and reshape their internal objects. Clinging to objects in the outside world or to frozen and immovable imagos, such patients labour indefatigably and painfully, like Sisyphus, in order not to let go the thread of the few cathexes which supply a frame for their distressed state of being. Is this a pathology of the extremes, or boundaries, of the analytic field? Yes, indeed. However, we should also recognize that analytic listening more and more frequently uncovers such features, woven into the fabric of so-called 'normal' organizations; they stand out as heterogeneous elements within seemingly neurotic constellations, or may finally emerge as a constitutive brushstroke on the canvas of personalities who appear as if graven in a polyptych.

While this pathology is, of course, narcissistic, it must be emphasized that it is quite impossible to link it today to any one specific clinical configuration.

1

Hope as a binding cathexis

Τοῖς δ ' ἐγώ ἀντί πυρός δώσω κακόν, ὦ
κεν ἅπαντες τέρπονται κατά υμόν ἐόν
κακόν ἀμφαγαπ ὦντες.

(Hesiod, *Works and Days*, lines 54–58)

As exemplified in the Pandora myth

Hesiod's *Works and Days*, one of the oldest of human attempts to synthesize the history of the cosmos and of mankind, is our source for the Pandora myth, which is woven into the fabric of the conflict played out between Zeus and Prometheus. Zeus the Olympian, king of the gods, ruling from the father's throne, angrily tells Prometheus, the son of Iapetos the Titan:

> You are pleased at having stolen fire and outwitted me – a great calamity both for yourself and for men to come. To set against the fire I shall give them an affliction in which they will all delight as they embrace their own misfortune[1]

(lines 54–58)

Affliction it may be, but they will delight in it as they embrace their misfortune, which lies concealed within their hearts. They will delight in an affliction, a misfortune. It is Pandora who will be sent to mankind through Epimetheus, as a present from Zeus, a homologue to Prometheus's gift.

But who is Pandora? According to Hesiod (*Works and Days*, lines 60–64), she was fashioned from earth and water by Hephaestus, who breathed into her a human voice and strength; she was modelled in the image of immortal goddesses, who endowed her with every charm and wisdom. However, Hermes, the messenger bringing her to Epimetheus, places in her breast lies, wily pretences and a knavish nature. Her name, which

5

means 'all gifts', has a twofold connotation: it refers to the gods who have contributed to this panspermia of afflictions, and also to herself as the bearer of all the spites that will befall mortals.

In the *Theogony* Hesiod tells how Pandora was created as an affliction for mankind to set against the fire (line 570), and that Zeus caused this beautiful bane to emerge[2] in the place of a blessing ('καλόν κακόν ἀντ' ἀγαθοίο ἐξαγαγ'', lines 585–586).

However, Pandora is by no means solely the woman created for the misfortune of men, as Hesiod presents her. In her form as the bearer of gifts, she is heiress to Pandoteira (she who gives all), one of the epithets of the earth goddess. As Anesidora, another name for the chthonic and agricultural power, she causes gifts to be brought up from the depths. This conception of Pandora is attested by her representation on a krater dating from 450 BC (in the Ashmolean Museum at Oxford): by a hammer blow, Epimetheus causes Pandora to emerge from a chasm in the earth. This is the theme of the *anodos*. Above, a little Eros flies towards Epimetheus. In this tradition, Pandora is a divinity of the earth and of fertility.[3] Furthermore, Pandora is the mother of Pyrrha, who married Deucalion, the son of Prometheus, and thereby became the mother of humankind.

Mechanisms of reversal and externalization operate in Hesiod's version of the myth, so that we no longer see Pandora arising from the depths of the earth which she personifies, containing evil which is within her. The Pandora shown to us holds a jar, which she has unstopped (πίθου μέγα πῶμ' ἀφελοῦσα),[4] thus releasing the grim cares inflicted by the gods on mankind. The punitive agency is here absorbed by the gods; the need for this projection becomes evident if we consider that the myth is connected in more than one respect with notions of transgression, seduction, secrecy and voyeuristic curiosity. As for the ambivalence, it emerges in connection with the gift – both Prometheus' gift to man and the gift of Zeus – even if the manifest text presents the two aspects as split, with Prometheus distributing bountiful gifts to man.[5]

In the Pandora myth, not only Epimetheus but also Pandora is inescapably punished: Pandora for having sought to see what was forbidden to her, and Epimetheus for having ignored the advice of his brother Prometheus, who had warned him that no gift from Zeus should ever be accepted. In this respect, the very formulation of the myth may be seen as psychoanalytic: Epimetheus gives no thought to what Prometheus has told him; he forgets, and, having accepted the gift, he had the bane before he realized (ὅτε δή κακόν εἶχε, νόησε)[6] what was happening.

Epimetheus, the antithetical double of Prometheus, accepts Pandora into his space because he fails to remember; he has repressed his brother's words. Knowledge of the evil harboured within remains the prerogative of Prometheus, linked as he is in the maternal line of descent to the chthonic goddesses, whose power of prophecy he possesses. Epimetheus, for his part, will understand later, as it were by deferred action. Epimetheus thus introduces us simultaneously to the thinking which follows the act and to the aftermath of a myth (epimithion). What will come after this myth, which I see as one of disclosure, is the making of the first human couple by Pyrrha and Deucalion, the children of Prometheus and Epimetheus, respectively.[7] Hence we have moved from the double to the couple along the route of disclosure and of acquired knowledge; the entire course of man's psychosexual development is to be found here.

Depths and the knowledge of what lies within them: that is the road on which Prometheus and Pandora meet. But there is another road too, that of hope, which Pandora detains in the 'unbreakable' prison of her jar. Hope is what remains to her, once the afflictions have been unleashed upon the world. Detained by her – or in her – hope is here connected with what lies concealed in the obscure depths. Prometheus, on the other hand, will allow it to wing its way to men. In Aeschylus's play, he will say: 'I placed in them blind hopes.'[8] By an omnipotent impulse, he presents himself as the one who grants (δοτήρ) all knowledge, and thereby 'caused mortals to cease foreseeing doom'. This was a mistake for which he will subsequently acknowledge his guilt (ἑκών, ἑκών ἥμαρτον[9] οὐκ ἀρνήσομαι). He will pay dearly for his 'fault', being chained by Zeus to the rock.

The gods keep what gives men life concealed. 'Zeus concealed it,' says Hesiod,[10] 'angry because Prometheus's crooked cunning had tricked him.' However, once the seed of fire has been stolen, Prometheus will place it in a fennel stalk; he is portrayed on another krater (Oxford, Ashmolean Museum, 420–410 BC), watching satyrs dancing with their torches and holding the narthex (fennel stalk) from which dazzling flames issue.

Whereas Prometheus sends hope among men, Pandora detains it in a box or jar. For me, Prometheus and Pandora may be regarded as each other's doubles, so that the order of the two myths can be imagined as reversed, with that of Pandora, the chthonic power, preceding that of the demigod, whose career can be deduced from his maternal line of descent. Through pain, renunciations and the quelling of passions, Prometheus will progress to his ultimate role of bearer of the flame.[11]

Prometheus sent hope among men, but hope is truly not always a boon to him who nurtures it. Jean-Pierre Vernant[12] treats the themes of Prometheus and Pandora as two aspects of one and the same story – that of 'human wretchedness . . . the need to toil upon the earth . . . to be born, to die, to have each day both the fear and the hope of an uncertain morrow'. The hope detained by Pandora in the obscure depths of her bodily jar surely has to do with the representation and the fear of the maternal power, as well as with the nostalgia of waiting for it to become available.

Owing to the range of desires and prohibitions to which both men and women are heir, the two aspects of the image of woman and mother are necessarily inherent in human thought. One is that of the archaic mother who irrevocably wields omnipotent power. Because she is the potentially destructive woman of the shadows, the dangerous and perverse seductress,[13] hers is the domain of the dark continents and of nameless horrors. Note that Hesiod uses the word πίθος for Pandora's jar. Now the πίθος, in the form of a large earthen vessel, was also used as a container for mortal remains, a place of interment. By unstopping her πίθος, the jar that is also a tomb, Pandora unleashed affliction, disease and death upon mankind. Here the emphasis is on the dark face of the power of Mother Earth.

The other face is that of fertile womanhood, receptive to luminous warmth, the bearer of life, helpful and protective, whose gentle availability affords protection from the terror of asphyxiating and annihilating attacks and banishes devouring anxieties. For this reason, the earth goddess often takes the form of the Core (κόρη) in the theme of the *anodos* (emergence). I believe that this is intended to represent not only renewal but also avoidance of the implications of the 'full' maternal form. Jane Harrison[14] notes that a kylix in the British Museum depicts Pandora both with that appellation and with her other name, Anesidora (she who causes gifts to emerge), which, as we know, denotes the earth goddess.[14]

In our fantasies, the two faces of woman and of mother have retained their magical or divine power. After an interval of thousands of years, in a land close to the one where the Pandora myth arose, the *Akathist Hymn* (the 'standing hymn')[15] transferred the hopes of all Byzantine Orthodox Christianity on to the figure of Mary, the Christian mother of the light of the spirit. According to Toynbee,[16] Mary, the human mother of Jesus, bided her time before taking the place of Isis and Cybele as the mother of a god (Theotokos).

However, in my view this Mary, the mother of the god who created everything[17] – father and son in the unity of the very spirit said to have come upon Mary[18] – has absorbed within her many attributes of the fertility goddesses. Notwithstanding all the interposed figures, a subterranean but ultimately unbroken thread links Gaia, the first divinity to have emerged from chaos, the single mother (prior to the incestuous seducing mothers), one of whose descendants is Pandora, to the Mary of Christian prayers.

Hail (Χαῖρε) Mary. But the Χαῖρε of the Byzantine hymns not only implies veneration, but also has the connotation of 'rejoice'. Is this a mnemic echo of a pleasure from another time – a pleasure buried, unrecognized, preserved in the bushy shadows of the oft-denied route linking the Mediterranean basin and Ancient Greece to Byzantium? At any rate, in order for the woman to become mother, sexual pleasure must be

8

forgone. The Virgin Mary condenses within herself all the prohibitions on the sexual life of the woman and mother. The *Akathist*, an anonymous hymn, is dedicated to the Virgin Mary. It is generally attributed to Romanos Melodos, who lived in the sixth century AD. Other possible authors are also mooted, dating it back to the fourth century AD, or alternatively forward to the eighth or even the ninth century AD.[19]

The hymn forms part of morning mass for the Saturday of the fifth week of Lent. It has been connected with specific historical events, with attacks by Byzantium's enemies during the reigns of Heraclius I, Constantine IV or Leo III (Isaurian dynasty). The people in the churches and on the ramparts of Constantinople sang:

> O Champion General, I your city now inscribe to you
> triumphant anthems as the tokens of my gratitude,
> being rescued from the terrors, O Theotokos.
> But since you have the dominion unassailable,
> from all kinds of perils free me so that unto you,
> I may cry aloud: rejoice, O Bride unwedded (Χαῖρε, νύμφη,[20] ἀνύφευτε).

Much later, C. Paparrigopoulos could still write that, for the (Greek) nation under the (Turkish) yoke, the *Akathist* mass 'unites spiritually what violence has scattered, and continues to fill our hearts with hopes for a better future'.[21] According to T. Xydis, the words of the *Akathist*:

> bear messages from another time. Like the frescoes of a Byzantine monastery, they transmit an ancient fear (δέος), which, however, is still relevant today insofar as it is one with the minds of the people around. This voice awakens our memories. Even if the concept of God is not readily accessible to us today, the words strike home in us unfailingly. And if the day should chance to come when this hymn is but the song of an obsolete creed, its poetry will yet live on unageing'.[22]

> The only hope of the hopeless[23]
> Spotless chamber of the Word
> Seashell that produces the divine pearl
> All-laudable Mother
> With your milk you nourished him who with a nod nourishes the entire universe
> Rejoice,[24] O bride unwedded
> Rejoice, height that is too difficult for human thought to ascend
> Rejoice, depth that is too strenuous for Angels' eyes to apprehend
> Rejoice, fiery throne of the Sovereign of all

My every hope I place in you, Mother of God, keep me under your protection

The Marian cult certainly does not date from the beginnings of Christianity. It arose during the centuries that followed the coming of Jesus, as the figure of Mary came to be increasingly glorified. The merciful mother, all gentleness, all light, all tenderness and all love – she is surely the ideal mother whom the child constructs for himself in earliest infancy. Untouched and untouchable by desire, a figure split off from all sexual reality, devoid of ambivalence and pure, she is the ever-virgin mother (Parthenos).

As Dominique Stein succinctly puts it, this is the negation of the primal scene.[25] But, of course, only a mother ideally excluded from the common destiny of women, an inaccessible object free from the realities of her human nature, could be the mediatress of all grace between the people and its God, fulfilling its hopes and delivering mankind from its afflictions – those afflictions for which Pandora, like Eve after her, is held responsible. One of the world's most beautiful songs, the *Akathist Hymn*, with which we are precisely concerned here, praises her glory and testifies that even God cannot do without a mother. As the mother upon whom all hopes converge, she represents Heraclitus's quest for the unhoped for; she is unavoidable and unapproachable, except in the expectation of her revelation.

Pandora's jar is the depository of maternal omnipotence in its two aspects of the giver of life and of death, and hope is a winged creature, a part-object kept enclosed and imprisoned by and within it. The myth could be said to equate hope, the penis and the promise of a child, which the mother, the origin of all life, retains for her own satisfaction or takes back into herself.

In the hands of Prometheus, the part-object loses its fleshly integument and becomes a feeling, which he implants in the hearts of men for their happiness and their doom. It will ultimately assume the form of a binding cathexis, as transferred on to the figure of the beneficent mediatress, Mary.

As exemplified in a patient's progress

Catherine came to me at the age of 38 because of a major disruption of the equilibrium that had hitherto prevailed in the relationship with her husband. After six years of marriage, the couple had separated in circumstances of physical violence, and Catherine spoke to me at length about her extremely anguished sadomasochistic relationship with her husband. It was a repetition of others of the same kind which had pervaded her life both as a girl and as an adult woman, the roots of which could easily be traced back to the relationship with her father.

Her difficulties were presented in the form of experiences of castration: inability to express herself, to find solutions, to take decisions, to progress in her career (in the behavioural sciences), to tackle the problems of her relations with her husband, parents, friends, and so on. There were indications of more serious difficulties in the background. Catherine said that she was unable to maintain friendships or love relationships; her reactions seemed to be determined mainly by her imaginary life, by her projections and splits. Her friends had little tolerance of her harsh and incessant criticism.

She complained of an impoverished intellectual life, although she had a good degree. She could not 'think properly'. People and things ultimately left her cold. She felt herself to be 'in a desert', dried up, often cut off from familiar places and from contact with those near to her. The world changed, but she did not. She felt secure only within the four walls of her house, where she would remain for hours on end without doing anything, without a thought in her head and devoid of interest.

She mentioned states of great agitation and 'excitement that sometimes mounted to an intolerable pitch', followed by a sense of exhaustion. She gave me a good demonstration of this during the preliminary interviews, in the form of violent fits of weeping; these were often to be repeated later, on the couch. She spoke, too, of another state, in which everything seemed 'tasteless' to her and she felt 'out of tune' with other people. She was different from them, like an alien, and then had to make a huge effort to follow what was going on around her. When in these situations, what she called 'her control' became meaningless for her. 'Like the limits', she said in the third interview, 'which you mentioned when you said I perhaps wanted to limit my analysis.' (She had told me in the first interview that she intended 'to have a year of analysis'.) What she expected from the analysis was the unblocking of her thought, the possibility of stopping the repetition of the failed relationships she had always had so far. She told me that she thought uninterruptedly, and constantly analysed herself, just as she unremittingly analysed other people's behaviour.

Catherine spoke of her mother, who was very attached to her own family on her father's side; she was often away from home, as she visited her own adored parents and siblings every day.

The patient's relationship with her father, who was himself very devoted to his own mother, was far from satisfactory. However, she had a few memories from the early years of her childhood: of a couple she had experienced as 'beautiful' and who made her very sad when they went out. But what predominated in her account were violent scenes between her parents: how she had often found her mother in tears and tried to comfort

11

her. She said that her mother took very little notice of her except when she was ill.

And Catherine had often been ill. She had had tonsillitis; a kidney disease about which she remembered little, except that, for two or three years, she had had to wear a boned corset that constricted her body and was very painful; and severe skin allergies. Later, she had always had period pains, and there were a spastic colon, diarrhoea alternating with constipation, episodes of fever, and low resistance to illness in general. She had been anorexic during her childhood.

The patient's mother figure was drastically split, the different elements being reflected in the two grandmothers. The same applied to the two grandfathers, one of whom appeared as a persecuted persecutor, and the other as affectionate, jovial and easygoing.

She had at one time felt very close to her father. It was during a period when her parents had separated. She was living with her mother in her maternal grandparents' house, but often visited her father. She would then sleep in her mother's old bed, which was still in the matrimonial bedroom, and she could remember the pleasure of snuggling up to her father and listening to the stories he would tell her. Then the parents lived together again. The relationship difficulties continued and Catherine felt alone, lost in the big house, filled with terror whenever either parent came back late. She had but one desire: to be free, to go far away, to leave home.

During the preliminary interviews, Catherine stared at me inscrutably, her features drawn, and I felt basically quite ill at ease; I sensed that she had within her a pronounced capacity (and a pronounced wish?) to suffer. And also to inflict suffering, as was to become evident later, during the course of the analytic work.

Listening to her speak, I was, of course, aware of the hysterical aspect and the exhibitionistic tendencies of her 'being different', her wish to control and her obsessional propensities. However, I also felt that the problem of limits and of control was very important to her, as she manifestly had a sense of being deprived of her own limits, both by the large cast of characters who invaded her, and in moments of fusion in which she said 'I' when referring to significant people in her life, such as her mother or her husband. Ultimately, she was no one and everyone at the same time. Later, during the analysis, she was often to say: 'Who am I? A nobody. Have I ever been anything else? I have no solid foundation, no point of reference.'

And indeed, notwithstanding the indications of sadomasochism, the patient suffered from a sense of being unable to commit herself, even in such relationships: 'I am there, but I am not.'

For all the difficulties, her speech was not impoverished, and so, in spite of her propensity to act out, I decided to take her in analysis, because I sensed a genuine suffering and because she was able during the preliminary interviews to associate to some of my remarks.

In the first year of the analysis, the patient had much to say about her father's 'vile' sadism and voyeurism, his meanness and his hatred of any man who came close to his daughter. She recalled her horrified fascination when a female cousin who had lived with them for a while screamed at the blows rained on her by her father for having gone out a few times secretly. She herself was later to receive the same token of his interest when he discovered her relationship with her husband-to-be.

The father had agreed to his daughter's marriage very reluctantly, but the young couple's relationship quickly deteriorated and they decided to part. Catherine said she was pleased not to have any children.

During her teens, my patient's attitude to the members of her family evidently swung from one extreme to the other. Sometimes her feelings were imbued with massive violence which she made no effort either to conceal or to control, whereas on other occasions they were, as she expressed it, 'soft'. She would then put up with everything, always give way, and closely follow her mother's religious activities. In the former phases, she would inflict her disparaging anxiety on everyone around her, with merciless verbal attacks (what she called 'flagellation in words'). Afterwards she would be overwhelmed with shame and guilt, which led her to act out by banging her head against doors, heaping insults upon herself, and finally sinking down in a heap, deprived of all her strength, devastated, drained and, as she herself said, immobilized on every level. In the other phases, she 'loved' everyone and nothing unleashed her aggression. Significantly, each swing was accompanied by a feeling of unfamiliarity with the previous phase. She knew what had happened, but there was as it were no longer any sense of having really experienced it.

Catherine thought that her mother had always remained insensitive to her pain, that she did not even suspect what her daughter was suffering. Incidentally, she herself was at first much more concerned about her aggression than about the pain concealed behind it.

In late adolescence and adulthood, she had totally uncensored dreams of homosexual scenes with her mother. However, Catherine had never had any actual homosexual relations. At twenty, she had been deeply in love with a young man, but owing to external circumstances the relationship had not developed.

The analysis was pervaded by periods of intense regression, during which she told me that her head was buzzing and on fire, her thoughts tumbling over each other. Her thoughts and words would have an almost diarrhoea-like, hypomanic flow. At these times, oral greed towards me rose to a devouring pitch, and there was little sign of guilt. She would say: 'I'm talking, I'm talking; I'm hungry.'

The sessions were punctuated by tears and complaints about being unable to forge links with people and to work. She repeated that she had nothing good inside her, that she could not stand herself. She heaped every possible disparaging epithet on herself, and her devastated face confirmed her descriptions of her experience of pain: 'It is not a human pain . . . It is the lining on an inside that has been laid waste.'

She would sometimes describe an experience of mounting tension, coupled with a need for immediate masturbatory discharge, during which her pleasure was mingled with the pain of sinking her fingernails into her hands. She often in fact mentioned masturbation, in which she had indulged unremittingly since her adolescence, and which she claimed was unaccompanied by any fantasies. If she was excited, this meant that she also felt invaded by destructive rage. At such times, her verbal or physical attacks on herself were characterized by merciless brutality. Then would follow a kind of calm after the storm, which she called her 'moments of sinking and sagging', moments when she managed to convey to me a very convincing impression of dislocation or of draining away to the point of obliteration. This she dubbed 'the death in her life'. There remained nothing but silence.

Meanwhile, her superego emerged in all its cruelty, as well as her demanding ideals, so that, even if she succeeded in something, she would plunge into comparisons with what 'might have been', belittle her achievements, or rush to give an account of them to female friends whom she knew to be condescending or even aggressive towards her. Depression appeared whenever her idealized self-image faltered.

She was never satisfied with her achievements at work, which were indeed well below her potential. Her performance was undermined by three factors:

Shame: She accused herself of not being sufficiently committed to her work. 'I lose interest very quickly . . . I forget . . . I get tired. I cannot love what I am doing . . . that is understandable, because I was never loved.'

Guilt: 'My mother wanted to go to university. That was not allowed . . . The result: a failed life, full of peevish feelings and regrets.'

Fantasies of power shot through with exhibitionistic desires: From her earliest years she had had daydreams in which she was awarded prizes for extraordinary literary achievements; or she was recognized by her colleagues as a leader (I happened to hear from other sources that she really did have uncommon organizational skills and practical capabilities); or she was a Joan of Arc saving the country from dictators; and so on.

These three factors not only hindered her own performance but, coupled with the long-standing restraint of her own tendencies to reject others,

14

ultimately brought about situations in which her feelings were hurt. For example, people she had not seen for a while would fail to recognize her when they met. Or people did not pay enough attention to her when she spoke. Or she did not get what she asked for.

These situations fuelled repetitive, traumatic dreams which, although not rich in content, condensed her oral, anal and genital difficulties and experiences of castration. There were scenes of quarrels with female servants who had not prepared a meal; or she was not ready to receive her guests; or, although the table was laid, there was nothing to eat; and so on.

The shortcomings which assailed her in every field – social and professional success, friendship, love, 'strength' – were offset by the magic power she attributed to her thoughts, which poured out in a constant flow, in a whirl, a seeming analogon of masturbation, with the concomitant function of excluding the analyst and evacuating the work of analysis. The words spoken were forgotten from one session to the next – something she obviously experienced as yet another narcissistic wound.

Her dependence on me and her difficulties with separations alternated with periods in which everything was immaterial to her and she had so little interest in herself that her physical integrity was threatened. For example, she failed to have a fractured gas pipe repaired; she did not have the faulty brakes of her car seen to; and one day she took some medicine without reading the instructions and then had to have her stomach pumped out in hospital.

For a long time she could make absolutely no sense of her apathy and lethargy, and of the depression that followed her fits of destructive rage. Other splits were maintained between her feelings during the sessions and the sequences of affects outside them.

The role she generally assigned to me was that of a binding agent: it was up to me to forge links between what happened during the sessions and from one session to the next, between past and present, between her thoughts and her knowledge of herself, which, no sooner gleaned, faded away, and between her dreams and her real-life activities. The way she received my interpretations denoted the existence of a threatening object that had to be annihilated as soon as it was cathected. There was no doubt in my mind that Catherine had to bring the analytic situation under the umbrella of her omnipotence,[26] but the transference implications of her current experience remained alien to her.

It seemed obvious to me that the question of psychic organization was also important. Winnicott reminds us that not everyone can have deep regressions.[27] The multifaceted organization of this patient was easy to detect: it had hysterical and obsessional aspects, as well as fundamental borderline characteristics with deficiencies in mental functioning whereby the soma was insufficiently protected. Her regressive experiences were

15

manifestly defensive in nature. However, I had many questions about the regular, virtually identical alternation of the regressive phases, their content and the rhythm of their repetition. How did she experience these regressions? What role did she assign to me in them? What factors were involved? How did she emerge from them?

What 'brought her out of her holes', as she put it, was not the content of my interpretations. As I soon came to realize, it was the fact of hearing my voice. She had to make me come out of my silence. While causing me to function as an auxiliary ego, she was plainly trying to control me, as well as to assure herself that I still existed, and, in particular, existed outside herself. For quite a while, I more or less acceded to her demand, which was connected with a thought that she disclosed to me much later: 'If she (the analyst) speaks, my hope is fulfilled.' It became possible to speak of hope only after the third year of her analysis.

Meanwhile, Catherine had succeeded in driving everyone away. She had no other relationship than the one she laboriously maintained with me; some tentative associations with men had gone awry. As soon as she began to go out with a man, she would become so possessive and would so idealize him that he would take to his heels, or, if he stayed, *she* would very quickly lose interest. As to the patient's sex life, she resorted anew to the anorexia of her childhood.

Was this the price she had to pay to be able to stay with me? Yes, but that was not all. A degree of guilt was, of course, involved, but, much more importantly, any request from another, however straightforward, was experienced by Catherine as an intrusion, a demand which stripped her of her strength, a threat to her integrity. Object withdrawal would follow.

She had all but given up her work; she did not want to 'clutter herself with friendships', and I was really made to feel that it was impossible for her to change anything in a life which caused her intense suffering. It was at this time that she told me of her hope.

> For a long time I have been hiding my expectation from you. I have always lived in hope. What of? I cannot tell you, because it is hope itself that counts for me now.
> When I was little I used to close my eyes tight and say to myself: just wait and it will come. In those days I wanted lots of things, but I did not make any effort. I was full of my hopes. Later, I still hoped that things would sort themselves out . . . I always had hope within me.
> Now I have nothing left and I am still hoping. Is it because I trust you? I certainly expected a lot from this analysis. Yet, things are only getting worse . . . But I carry on hoping. . . . That feeling of hope is there, buried in the deepest recesses of myself. I did not even want to talk to you about it. . . . What possible understanding could you have of it all?

For me, it is my welfare. Something not to be shared. Telling you about it would take all the flavour out of it. . . . As if I were going to lose it. . . . As if you were depriving me of it.

If I let things happen to me, I shall have nothing left. If I do anything myself, my state of hope will also be gone. Let me stay motionless. Nurture it in myself. . . . I love my hope. I will not change it for anything. . . . In my suffering, I can still hope.

Catherine was thus preserving a narcissistic space for herself, which was felt to be threatened by cathexis of the analyst.

I shall not here describe the progress of the analysis, or attempt to show how my patient and I gradually succeeded in laying the foundations for the eventual construction of a screen revealing two existences recognized as separate but in relation with each other. Nor shall I discuss the pain of my countertransference, except to say that I too often felt caught up in a tendency to project the rejection of my interpretative activity into a fertile 'future'.

My interest will centre on the place of hope in Catherine's psychic economy – as a resistance and as the shield of her narcissism – and this will be the subject of the second part of this book. First of all, however, some theoretical background is necessary, to afford a better understanding of the dynamic and economic factors underlying the operation of hope in this patient.

Clinical and metapsychological background

On cathexes

Freud's thinking on the problems of psychic energy and cathexes followed as it were by deferred action from two observations: that what excites is cathected, and that the need may be satisfied, whereas this is not the case with the pressure stemming from the internal thrust of the desire. This means that there are movements which place the psychic apparatus under tension and which are the expression of an inner force, called a 'drive', itself resulting from the transformation of somatic excitations.[1] This tension and its consequences arise in relation to the exciting entity and to what is desired. Interaction and the relation with the object are therefore immediately involved. This force is also implicated in the work of psychic transformations in their manifold guises. The psyche is work because its operation is governed by the drives, on which it in turn labours since they are a constant charge and the mind cannot escape from them. It may try to rid itself of them or elaborate them by binding the excitations to representations, affects, objects in the external or internal world, and various experiences and situations.

This binding work may be understood as a charge of positive or negative energy cathexes – a quota of psychic energy – applied to objects and the external world, to the body or to the psychic morphemes and the agencies, such as the ego. In the realm of drive energy, libidinal cathexis corresponds to cathexis by the energy of the sexual drives.

This conception was left intact by the radical change in Freud's thought that occurred in the 1920s, except that, once again by deferred action – in this case following his reflections on some clinical failures – he was led to postulate the parallel action of a thrust opposed to that of the libidinal energy; this thrust is known, not very aptly for some, as the death drive.[2]

It has been suggested that the choice of the terms 'life drive' and 'death drive' in the second theory is attributable to a jump to the most philosophical level of the mystery of life and death, and that this gives rise to confusions between psychoanalysis and biology, between the conditions of psychic life and those of the life of the organism as a whole.[3] Freud certainly expected a great deal from biology as a proving ground for his theories (1920g, p. 60), but he nevertheless placed the erotic and destructive impulses squarely in the domain of analysis – that is, in psychic territory. To describe the death drive, he adduced concepts such as masochism, unconscious guilt, the negative therapeutic reaction and the repetition compulsion. Analysts today can therefore set aside the biologizing parameters, and concentrate on Freud's concern to express by the term 'death drive' the ideas of inertia and anaesthesia in the psychic apparatus, as well as tendencies for drives to become defused trends of decathexes.

They may also espouse G. Rosolato's view that the term 'death drive' compels psychoanalytic theory to embark on the risky venture of maintaining the biological and somatic, or simply material, references by transposing them into organizations of meaning and psychic conflicts.[4] The fact that this operation concerns the thought of death has several implications. It evokes fusion with sexuality, internalizations, the deployment of paradoxes and the link with repetition; so that, on the one hand, psychoanalysis takes on a particular originality and, on the other, the mythical dimension of the death drive is clearly brought out. If death is stated to be a drive, this means that it is transferred from the external to the internal world (both biological and psychic), and we can then begin to conceive of the work performed in collaboration with the life drive.

We can, of course, reject the use of the death drive concept in both theory and practice, and some analysts have not hesitated to do so.[5] However, it seems to me that we thereby deprive ourselves of the dynamic conception which reduces the conflict to its most elementary level – i.e. that of cathexes and decathexes of drives, as well as of the force that tends to tear psychic unities apart. Again, the use of a term which covers all trends opposing the mind's erotic and aggressive libidinal cathexes preserves the idea of a basic conflict that is present even in the absence of any pathology, as Freud points out in his paper on negation.

At any rate, we know that the death drive cannot be encountered in the pure state, either as drive or as death. Freud from the outset emphasized the capture of the death drive by the libido, thereby espousing the idea of erotogenic masochism – i.e. of a level where a degree of fusion is always present, this being essential to the very existence of psychic life and thought (Rosenberg, 1982). The important point, however, in my view is the Freudian notion of a force of pure negativity, which is opposed in the mind to the positiveness of the life drives; after all, Eros for Freud is not the exact equivalent of the sexual drive but is a force which produces and preserves unities (Freud, 1920g, pp. 60–61). In naming the death drive, Freud wished to draw our attention to a force responsible for the negative trends observable in patient and analyst alike, which sets limits to the possibilities of treatment and also presents obstacles to thought and theorization (Potamianou, 1989, p. 929).

With regard to the pathology of borderline states, the alternation between phases of cathexis and of decathexis is particularly important both quantitatively and qualitatively, as we are faced here not with mere swings between movements of cathexis, decathexis and recathexis or counter-cathexes, but with phases of decathexis during which energy is delibidinalized, so that the pleasure principle is put out of action.

Delimiting cathexes and cathexes of limits

In his paper on the neuropsychoses of defence (1894a, p. 60), Freud defined cathexes as sums of excitation capable of increase, diminution, displacement and discharge, spread over the memory traces of ideas. At this point in his career, Freud was therefore linking cathexes with the activity of representations. He never abandoned this viewpoint, even if representation was no longer one of his central concerns in the second theory: in his *Moses* (1939a [1934–1938], p. 97), he was still distinguishing between conscious, preconscious and unconscious ideas and representations according to the distribution of the psychic energy of cathexes. The same position is evident in the *Outline* (1940a [1938], p. 164), in which Freud adds: 'we [. . .] even venture to suppose that a hypercathexis [of psychical material] brings about a kind of synthesis of different processes – a synthesis in the course of which free energy is transformed into bound energy'. When energy is bound to images, representations and substitutive constellations, such as symptoms, the psychic apparatus is relieved of excitations, while still controlling the flow and discharge of energy.

Freud had already foreshadowed three essential characteristics of cathexes in the *Project* (Freud, 1950c [1895]):

1 Their combined endogenous and exogenous origin (the problem of drives versus perceptual data).
2 Their nature as a reserve of energy. (The question of its location – in the ego or the id, or perhaps in an at first undifferentiated id-ego – was to be tackled later.)
3 Their organizing and delimiting function. Freud writes (p. 323): an organization has been formed in ψ (i.e., impermeable neurones) whose presence interferes with passages [of quantity] . . . . This organization is

called the '*ego*' . . . . Thus the ego is to be defined as the totality of the ψ cathexes, at the given time, in which a permanent component is distinguished from a changing one.

The last of these points calls in my opinion for particular emphasis; the first two have already been the subject of much discussion in the psychoanalytic literature. The use of the word 'distinguished' is a reference to the delimiting organizing function of binding cathexes. If these are sufficient, there will be relative stability, allowing the alternation in the process of cathexis–decathexis–recathexis that is essential for free circulation between the three agencies of the mind, the id, the ego and the superego. This also ensures that the structures/morphemes organized within the psychic apparatus can be maintained, whether this possibility is seen in terms of agencies, of their productions (representations/affects concerning external or internal objects; the self; enactments in fantasy; etc.), or alternatively of levels of functioning. For example, it is the existence of memory elements sufficiently cathected at the unconscious level that renders possible the constituent recathexis of what is known in psychoanalysis as representation.

We know that these memory traces are 'of mixed race', involving the coexistence of perceptual elements, selected in accordance with whatever constituted a psychic stimulus, and excitations from the body, albeit transformed at psychic level. These traces are signs of what has captured the drive charges, and for precisely this reason their cathexis defines their position and boundaries in psychic life. When recathected, they will become representational elements, whose organization may then change both qualitatively and quantitatively.

By virtue of its function as psychic work on the relationship of presence/ absence – what was formerly there but is no longer – representation is the mark of a cathexis that occupies the ground between the two. It therefore delimits a field which separates what could be attached to the fact of two presences. In this process, however, the representational morpheme – which is an articulation of signs either accompanied by, or separated from, their affective charge – establishes another limit on the boundaries of the representational gap.[6]

At the other end, by raising the process of cathexis to a higher level (i.e., by hypercathexis),[7] the reality principle and thought ultimately assert themselves. The action of repression is triggered by the demand for cathexis of traces whereby ideas are judged as true or false by comparison with the memory traces of external reality. In releasing the energy bound to it, the repressed element not only permits new forms, serving as countercathexes, to emerge but also delimits the field of action of the objects of desire. The destiny of excitations thus proves to be determined by the framework of a psychic organization which, by preventing the free outflow of energy and abrupt discharges, facilitates displacements and condensations.[8]

Freud always insisted (1916–17f [1915], p. 235; 1920g, pp. 30–31) that the lack or insufficiency of cathexes affects all systems and leaves the way open to the effects of excitations. His conception of trauma introduces the notion of an invasion of the psychic apparatus by uncontrolled excitations. The mind can defend itself against these only if it is capable of supplying large quantities of countercathexes around and on the margins of the traumatic breach, or if it can discharge the excess excitation to the outside. Failing this, the apparatus is flooded and the pleasure principle is put out of action (1920g, p. 29). It is important to note that the demand for hypercathexis around the trauma has the consequence of impoverishing the other systems, so that other functions are substantially diminished in their efficiency or paralysed. If hypercathexis, which thus becomes 'cathexis against', impoverishes other psychic elements or sectors, then cathexes and countercathexes can be understood as delimiting and organizing activities, whereas the insufficiency or absence of cathexes constitutes a potential for disorganization. This delimiting and organizing tendency is manifest from the very dawn of psychic life and it affords the best approach to understanding the differentiation between agencies.

In his discussion of the concept of primal repression, which constitutes an epistemological reference and a functional necessity for secondary repression, Freud has the following to say about its mechanism (1915e, p. 181): 'Anticathexis is the sole mechanism of primal repression.' While primal repression can be seen as a defensive operation by an already existing ego, whose result is the binding of archaic defences, such a position has certain implications, as I have previously shown.[9] If, on the other hand, primal repression is seen as giving rise to the separation of the id and ego systems, a different approach becomes possible to the problem of this countercathexis, which cannot come from the ego as it is its founder.

Freud refers in this connection to representations which have not received cathexes on the preconscious level. If we assume that the drive charges are not initially distributed in separate systems, it may be postulated that, since decathexis is not involved, the factor that will give rise to the first elementary internal perception of differences is the cathexis of certain traces which have different effects on the rudimentary psyche – dysphoric on the one hand and satisfying on the other – by a crude energy.[10] Two kinds of experience of the self, which is not yet distinguished from the mother's body, are perceived here. These perceptual elements may therefore well trigger the beginning of a type of psychic functioning that will seek protection from unpleasure by placing a greater charge on the rudiments of traces that oppose it; in other words, certain representational elements will be hypercathected and their force will act against the others. This hypercathexis will then correspond to a countercathexis.

The 'different–contrary' traces, still permeated by the subject's own body and that of the mother, that drain a dysphoric experience are set aside by hypercathexis of other traces which afford a moderate pleasure. Hypercathexis, which becomes cathexis 'against', at the same time lays down the earliest foundations of the ego. In the later defensive operations of this agency, the first setting aside will assume the status and qualification of primal repressed material.

In my opinion, the recathexis of the traces of pleasurable experiences is the first sign of the work of a psychic apparatus attempting to get its bearings in a world without limits. In a previous contribution (1984), I described these elementary first experiences as demarcating,[11] because they are demarcated in the mind in two senses of the word: (a) they are outlined in the first experiences of life; and (b) the mark of their origin disappears, because they are not admitted into the (not yet constituted) preconscious system. Because they have not received any cathexis from the preconscious, it will never be possible for them to become conscious and accessible. However, they may well offer themselves as a point of fixation of the drive in the unconscious. Behind them lies the abyss of the non-representable, of that which cannot be given form, in which the drive may be imagined as functioning in the absence of ideational representatives.

As already stated, to counteract the first dysphoric elements, other elements of functioning in the well-tempered satisfaction of the infant's needs by the mother are hypercathected. During the mother's absences, they become the substrate for the psychic activity which, through hallucinatory satisfaction, will ultimately allow the differentiation of what will become the ego.

The first representational material to be repressed is therefore made up of the recathexes of traces, still permeated with the experience of the subject's own body and that of the mother; and the first countercathexis is a hypercathexis, which, by becoming a cathexis 'against', at the same time founds the ego through the setting aside of the cathected traces of certain dysphoric sensations. The latter will assume the status and quality of primary repressed material in the defensive operations of the ego.

It is perhaps worth recalling that, when Freud pointed out that repression directs countercathexes outwards, whereas regression modifies the ego by internal countercathexes, he noted that this proposition was not absolute. At any rate, he was here referring to a later period of life, when all elements of the organization of the agencies are in place.

A. Green (1983, p. 162) in turn comments that repression may be conceived of as performing a twofold function. Firstly, it keeps at bay object cathexes that might threaten the organization of the ego. Secondly, it constitutes an integument on its outer surface to set the limits with which it provides the ego. These limits are shifting, variable and of fluctuating permeability. Upon any serious threat to narcissism, they may tighten up, harden, or even turn into a shell. There is therefore a limiting function – or limit function – whereby repression becomes an ego function, both internally (relative to the id) and externally (relative to the reality of the object). Analytic experience shows that these two limits tend to merge into one, through projection. But how is the advantage afforded by the limit to outweigh the disadvantage of loss of the unlimited due to having separated what will henceforth be kept on either side of the limit – i.e., when a difference has been established?

In my view, difference becomes established precisely by the cathexis of representations of objects remote from consciousness which exist solely on the non-conscious level. Repression is obviously only one of the possible mechanisms of ego formation, but it is the pre-eminent organizing mechanism that ensures the stabilizing coherence of the ego as an agency, unlike others such as projection, splitting and disavowal.

In the model of the twofold limit, one barrier provides separation within the internal world, while another separates inside from outside, on both the psychic and bodily levels. Once again, this psychoanalytic model becomes understandable in terms of delimiting cathexes, while countercathexes or decathexes of the representations of objects, of self or of external reality, as well as of bodily reality, reinforce or undermine the efficacy of binding cathectic activity.

In psychoanalytic terms, the external object in this connection has the function of an inducer and catalyst of binding operations whereby cathexes can be transferred on to internal psychic activity.[12] A meeting between subject and object therefore normally permits the organization of the primary processes on the basis of the pleasure–unpleasure polarity.

From the point of view of drive-binding operations, I consider that the internal object may be conceived of as a network of libidinal cathexes investing on three levels of functioning (unconscious, preconscious and conscious), while the ego also maintains cathexes with the external world. Since the network extends over different levels, its constitution proceeds by way of continuities and discontinuities, and the object comes into being as a result of the transformations occurring in the passage from level to level. As long as the pleasure principle holds sway, cathexes are organized under its aegis, giving rise to operations of displacement, condensation, reversal, inclusion and exclusion. When the reality principle takes over, it will govern these operations. It will then be possible to deal with continuities/discontinuities, presence and absence by means of word presentations in the field of language.

24

After 1920, this progression is no longer taken for granted in Freud's texts: the antagonism between drives now finds its true theatre in the object. P. Marty's recent concept of a fragmented unconscious [*inconscient parcellaire*] introduced a dimension that can be associated with this antagonism.[13]

If cathexis is regarded as a process of energy condensations designed to avoid free outflow and discharges that might drain and hence annihilate the psychic apparatus,[14] the question of the stability of cathexes and countercathexes arises in terms not only of the delimitation of ego and non-ego, or of the erotogenic zones of the body, as opposed to the limitlessness of symbiosis, but also of the capacity to maintain the cathexes and countercathexes of the limits themselves. On the one hand, this ensures that the frontier remains relatively intangible, while, on the other, it allows opposition among elements, without thereby ruling out their interpenetration.[15]

Integration of the various elements, on either side, depends on the upholding of the boundary system – i.e., the maintenance of a line of demarcation which separates the other from the same. At the same time the 'other', as a *heteron* of consciousness or of the object, of spaces or situations, is recognized in the defensive strategy of the ego,[16] which organizes its resistances in order to protect its homoeostasis. Conversely, if cathectic/countercathectic activity is shallow and excessively fragile compared with sudden upsurges of the drives, self-regulation of excitations is impaired, so that cathexes consume too much energy and are felt to be too painful. Everything tends to become traumatic, and all forms of functioning which delimit cease to facilitate the alternation of cathexes, decathexes and recathexes, and instead turn into a barrier to be obliterated – and hence into a rickety limit.

G. Painchaud and N. Montgrain have pointed out that the 'borderline' concept, as a state organized 'at the limits', can be understood in two ways.[17] On the one hand, it is delimited by neurosis and psychosis, while, on the other, it is that which is included in the frontier separating them. Being neither neurosis nor psychosis, it includes elements of both. Borderline patients do indeed use mechanisms which belong to both pathologies. However, what do we mean if we say that the borderline state stems from the non-integration of borderline experiences, because the ego maintains a position half-way between neurotic control and psychotic regression, and that acting out is an attempt to grasp a reality to which it clings?

The drive-related element of pleasure or suffering may present itself in the form of an unmediated excess, so that it does not appropriately connote the passage from outside to inside and vice versa, and therefore organizes boundary deficiencies. However, in my view the important point is that, irrespective of the possible explanations for this situation, borderline subjects ultimately organize themselves around the deficiencies in their capacity to maintain cathexes and countercathexes, and, in particular, to transfer them on to everything which establishes limits, both inside and outside.

Cathexes and decathexes in borderline states

Reflections and hypotheses

In 1989 I wrote about patients who seem compelled to reduce or even completely silence their mental functioning whenever the work of association in the analytic session (and outside too, when they can keep it up) introduces elements of perception and apprehension that mobilize their capacity to use thought for the purpose of linking affects to words and to the subject's experience, thereby making connections with his history.[18] This occurs when the patient begins to deploy new kinds of defences with the onset of changes in psychic functioning. At these moments the transference relationship can draw breath, because it is not threatened with invasion by intrusion and separation anxieties. These analytic phases are often followed by repetitions whose main objective is a discharge with a view to reducing to zero level the excitation that is disrupting mental work. The repetitions take the form of acting out and/or abrupt somatizations unaccompanied by any capacity to associate; they are frequently succeeded by phases of withdrawal, and finally by decathexis of self (body and thought) and of others. It is as if the introduction into the psychic economy of potentially transformative elements necessitated the immobilization or annihilation of mental functioning, so as subsequently to bring about a more general cathexis–reducing tendency, at least in some of these patients.

In such borderline analysands, the conflict may be deemed to be connected with change. Somatic discharges or episodes of acting out, and phases of withdrawal of cathexes, do indeed regularly burst into the analysis as soon as internal mobilization introduces into the subject's psychic field factors likely to change the internal imagos or the experience of an external reality. The same applies if the incipient new types of psychic functioning reveal the use of defences other than the customary ones of splitting, projection and the like.

As one male patient said, 'when certain known and familiar images or perceptions change, I get lost. Different images cannot survive in me, and I cannot even tolerate their alternation. If one image follows another, the first one is completely blotted out and disappears'. At such times he was invaded by terrible anxiety. He felt that he was sinking into quicksands, swamps, craters, what he called 'ulcerated' landscapes. He would dream of people who turned into monsters or sucked his blood like vampires. If I interpreted these images in transference terms and imparted meaning to the episodes which tended to sever all the moorings of our relationship, that seemed to have very little effect on the situation. Only the feeling of getting lost in repetitive discharges that left him exhausted allowed my analysand to recover at a later stage, when he would painfully try to understand and work through.

On the manifest level, such patients certainly dread changes and the unknown, which endanger their sense of control and their security system, while exposing the inadequacy of their capacity for accommodation and assimilation, appropriation and relationship with the 'other'.

One patient explained to me that space and time had to remain close to him and known, otherwise he would get lost. Nothing should move: that was his ideal. At home, everything had to remain immovable – objects, furniture, whatever. He felt that events registered in him, but that he could not integrate them within his linear experience of time.

The patient said:

> At that point I explode in rage and I set about destroying everything . . . I have to smash this reality, which intrudes into me like a cataclysmic wave, which swamps me and then retreats, leaving me inert, drained of all substance, of life and strength. There I cease to be anything at all, I feel nothing. It is as like being invaded by the void.

The 'new' is registered as something totally unknown, that makes things and situations unfamiliar, owing to the rifts, breaches and differentiations it introduces, which disturb the subject's narcissistic omnipotence.

Breaches in the known, in the familiar, in psychic reality as well as in external reality, which is experienced as if it were a reflection in a mirror, subvert narcissistic encystment, secrete panic and, depending on the individual, trigger manic defences, confusional states or, quite often, narcissistic withdrawal and decathexes of objects and self. It is as if the ego, deprived of the bearings afforded by daily routines devoid of surprises, or of familiar perceptions, feelings and behaviours, suddenly feels alienated from itself, invaded by disorganizing anxieties, at grips with the 'unfamiliar', as one female patient put it to me. The sense of the unfamiliar was due to the interposition of the unexpected between her and her world, which at such times she could no longer keep fixed and immutable. The unexpected, of course, had to do with anything that differentiated and demarcated itself, separated and thereby became unfamiliar. One patient said that if he wrote, the words turned into something unfamiliar for him, 'unrecognizable little bits'.

However, I do not think that change itself is the problem here. I contend that the issue in these patients is the dread of psychic mobilization, because it calls for more libidinal cathexes – i.e., expenditure on object-related and narcissistic binding of an energy they say they do not have, or whose expenditure they claim to experience as a draining of their being. After all, it is a matter of integrating into the ego new elements connected with modes of interaction with the external environment and with significant relations in intrapsychic reality, and hence of assuming cathexes that signal the difference between the known and the unknown, the foreseen and the unexpected, the old and the new.

At such times, of course, these patients have to accept the impossibility of having total control over the elements of external and internal reality, and of achieving the absolute possession to which they aspire. As my patient said: 'If I allow changes, I am no longer the master of things. Anything I am not certain of possessing becomes alien to me, and I then feel I am losing pieces of myself . . . I feel destroyed.'

The problem is solved by immediate discharges, which prevent the cathexis of memory traces that differ from each other. It seems to me that the reason is not a prohibition on the working of the psyche, which would suggest the idea of forbidden pleasure (although this aspect may also be present). In my view, the situation here is one of psychic mobilization calling for the displacement of libidinal cathexes on to differentiating, and hence also delimiting, elements. In order to avoid these cathexes, the psychic apparatus is compelled to resort to types of discharge which inevitably cause the work of thought to fail and which reveal the weaknesses of the psychic framework. That is to say, even if the ego and objects of these analysands do not succumb to experiences of confusion and non-differentiation, their psychic content (images, thoughts and feelings) seems at times to lose the ability to conform to spatial and temporal co-ordinates in a way that maintains a stable sense of ego cohesion and continuity.

When psychic mobilization bursts the internal frame asunder, there ensues instead a kind of framing of general activity by the automatic operation of those repetitions which substantially escape the pleasure principle.[19] Recourse to such repetitions is the ultimate barrier erected against psychic silence. These repetitions are movements against movement, because, in pursuing the identical, they preserve by freezing.

As we know, the dread of psychic mobilization affords an escape route from the dynamics of changes and of constructions/reconstructions. That is a truism. However, the point is that this organization dispenses with costly cathexes when the mind aims for 'constancy' and when this tendency towards constancy blocks the way to what Freud called the Nirvana principle.[20] What the borderline patient is ultimately resisting is not change or the object in itself (refusal of the object), but the expenditure of cathectic energy on unstable limits.

28

Any decathexes are neither those of neurotic strategy nor the more or less permanent ones that characterize psychosis; they are temporary, albeit repetitive, failures of the binding systems, due to the impossibility of maintaining constancy in the alternations of cathexes, decathexes and recathexes, when the mind is invaded by disorganizing anxieties while at grips with the unfamiliar.

This leads me to a second hypothesis. In my opinion, the conscious sense of the 'unfamiliar' corresponds to moments of possible compromise, when differentiating and separating factors give rise to a decathecting tendency, but the cathexes partially persist, whereas decathexis is introduced through the sense of loss of familiarity, and hence of binding contact. The difficulty of maintaining libidinal – object-related and narcissistic – cathexes is manifested in feelings of partial or complete loss of object and of self (unfamiliarity, detachment of pieces of flesh, outflowing, etc.). By contrast, the automatic operation of repetition guarantees a relationship with what has been lost.

The relevant cases show two main types of repetition, notwithstanding minor individual differences:

1 Repetitions in which the predominant factor is sudden discharge and the draining of excitations in acts and somatizations with virtually no potential for representation; here, it seems that there can be no eventual access to the integration of meaning. These repetitions are well beyond the pleasure principle as presented in the second theory of the drives. This does not mean that repetitions subject to the pleasure principle are necessarily absent in these cases.
2 Repetitions which manifestly involve a traumatic relation to the drive, to the extent that their aim is to re-experience painful losses.

The second type of repetition might be attributable to a well-known characteristic of borderline states, namely the alternation of loss and attempts at object recovery at the expense of external objects, or even of the subject's own body. This represents a desperate effort at reunion with an object within, even by way of the experience of its loss, and thereby at holding on to it. However, precisely this effort is thwarted by the fixation to the loss of the object; hence the traumatic relationship to the drive.

The first type of repetition thus involves loss at the level of manifestations of the dynamic unconscious, by obliteration of traces and also draining of intolerable excitations. In the second type of repetition, loss of the object, which is also a self, predominates. The loss of this object (a narcissistic one) is therefore countercathected. Fixation, as the link with what has been lost, is the final protective dam for the narcissistic cathexes, while two factors are at work in the mind: firstly, the tendency towards immobilization, which ensures that the productions of narcissistic omnipotence remain immovable; and secondly, the thrust towards silence through discharges intended to drain excitations to zero level.

The libidinal element is constantly in danger of disqualification in borderline subjects, owing, of course, partly to an uncontrollable quantitative excess, but also, I believe, to the defusion of drives, which leaves the mind exposed to the pressure of internal excitations, sustained and augmented by external ones. In a word, anticipation of representation and affect here proves to be deficient. It seems to me that the defusion of drives can also explain why borderlines confronted with uncontrolled libido leap upon the object, even if they then experience the pangs of intrusion/separation anxiety; or why, conversely, if they feel threatened by annihilating and self-destructive tendencies, they flee from excitations and often seek to reduce them to the lowest possible level. As one patient said, 'a slight increase in the level of internal or external excitations is liable to make everything fall apart'.

The analyst may choose to interpret repetitions in terms of fixations, and instances of non-binding in terms of libidinal insufficiencies. However, by confining ourselves to the role of fixations, we shall fail to account for the first type of repetitions discussed above. Equally, libidinal insufficiency, or narcissistic defences against the Oedipus complex or the psychic pain of separation, do not adequately explain the dynamic of those self-destructive processes in which masochism is de-eroticized.

In view of the repetitions we encounter in the cases I have discussed, and of the concomitant degradation of masochistic manifestations, we should remain open to the possibility of a conflict between a drive current making for binding and life, and another current opposing it.

The history of these patients, as remembered and/or reconstructed, may also reveal the non-internalization of a mothering agency, as Joyce McDougall noted. Whether one agrees with M. Fain and D. Braunschweig that this history is indicative of an inadequate protective shield against stimuli, or accepts my own theory that it betrays the failure of the ego to assume the function of watchfulness,[21] the fact is that these patients confront us with what I see as the dread of psychic mobilization, connected with what I shall call the anxiety of internal and external delimitations that demand cathexes and countercathexes. Intrusion and separation anxieties, as commonly described in object relations, seem to me to be of secondary importance compared with this anxiety concerning the delimitation of territories, both internal and external. This last hypothesis is, I think, proved by the mechanisms of projective identification and the incorporation of fantasies observed in these cases.

Behind the anal activity of retention/preservation and ejection/destruction lies a problem complex involving primary capturing anality,[22] in which the encystment of an immobilized and petrified nuclear part of the self that is moulded from infantile omnipotence protects the subject from being marked in any way by differences or distinctions (especially those between sexes and generations).

Intrusion and separation anxiety in relation to the object is connected with the aim of its total incorporation, as well as with the reversal of this aim in the horror that the object, by insinuating itself, might take possession of the subject's territory and threaten his omnipotence. This psychic reality is buried in order to preclude the threat. Under the pressure of the drives and dominated by infantile megalomania, the ego will brook no delimitation. Attacks on the psychic work of binding and on the analytic process are accompanied by an onslaught against the setting that is their vehicle. At such times the setting has to be destroyed, not only because it restricts omnipotence, but also because it contains the entire potential of the process.

Such an economy naturally calls for modifications of technique. To the extent that repetition not only serves the purpose of erosion of, or even of reunion with, the traumatic, but becomes the delimiting factor of a mind threatened with obliteration, it confronts the analyst with very specific problems of technique and functioning.

Delimitation anxiety

The ego in its internal/external relations

If the problem of the relations of borderline patients with their world can be defined as the search for specular conformity of objects, their external reality must be regarded as built up mainly from the projective activities of the ego. It should, however, be noted that these activities do not invade the psychic stage in the same way as in psychotics; the reality principle is not disabled here.

All authors agree that contact with reality and a more or less effective capacity on the part of the ego to cope with daily life are preserved, at least as long as situations that might encourage the emergence of the regressive potential do not arise. Most authors consider that the ego of borderline subjects is extremely vulnerable, and some even claim that it is on the verge of fragmentation. O. Kernberg (1975, p. 39), however, refers to an ego which has been able to develop its boundaries notwithstanding the disorders of relations with internalized objects and the predominance of primitive defences. It is therefore worth attempting a more accurate definition of the circumstances and moments when reality testing proves to be deficient.

Clinical psychoanalysis shows that, as long as external reality can still be managed so as to afford narcissistic satisfactions, there is little evidence of its rejection. However, the slightest sign of disappointment causes the same reality to become unacceptable. And disappointments do indeed abound, for narcissistic sensitivity is at all times manifest. One woman patient said that she often met friends in the street who did not immediately recognize her, a fact which she explained as follows: 'Of course, I am a person of no consequence. Why should they want anything to do with me? They do not see me; I do not exist for them.'

The capacity to act in order to modify disappointments is completely lacking in these subjects, who often give the impression of being passive participants in situations of privation, waiting for some magic deliverance. In unfavourable circumstances, they resort either to narcissistic withdrawal or to decathexis, and seek new objects and situations to cathect. Ultimately, the impetus for cathexes always appears to stem from objects and situations chosen for their 'sameness', in a specular relationship that knows nothing of differences and rejects distinctions.

Winnicott (1971, p.107) referred to objects which never become anything other than 'subjective' objects, because they have never been separated from and genuinely placed outside the subject. The concept of the self-object, which is so familiar to English-speaking authors, seems to me also to imply a conception of the world in which elements, like events, are treated as if they were part of the subject, the charge of whose projective activity they bear. In the absence of delusion, it is at least the case that external reality carries a powerful invasive and persecutory potential, confronting the subject with a reality that threatens his psychic integrity. One patient, for example, moved constantly from one apartment to another, because the plumbing problems he encountered each time made him feel persecuted by water. He was totally unaware of the projective process which dictated his reference to everyday reality.

In this context, the relationship of the ego to the oppositions of internal/external and inside/outside, which Freud (1915c) considers always to be characterized by rejection of the hated/unpleasurable and by retention of the pleasurable/loved, at the same time features a constant search for boundaries to be drawn between objects and the self, between internal and external perceptions; however, any boundary is immediately disputed, as it would create a separation between the subject and a world whose otherness he rejects. The ego is caught up in this dilemma and is unable for two reasons to assume its mediating role: firstly because it is constantly confronted with the danger of invasion and encroachment by an outside world which threatens its integrity, and, secondly because, being dependent on that world owing to the deficiencies in its own organization, it cannot declare its independence of it. Fixations to early traumas drive demands that outstrip the capacity of a defective shield against stimuli, and either an overabundance or a dearth of relations with primary objects: these are the factors generally adduced to describe the psychogenesis of an ego poor in narcissistic and libidinal energy, which is thereby compelled to seek anaclitic support from without.

The deficiencies of the ego are revealed by the impossibility of recourse to repression-based symptoms and to the depressive economy. The latter after all here has relatively little relevance to superego conflicts, but has to do mainly with the dangers to psychic or somatic integrity presented by the withdrawal of external supports, lack of self-esteem, asthenic experiences and the like. However, these deficiencies are in my view occasioned by the necessity to cathect – i.e., by an intrinsically delimiting activity. In particular, they result from cathexes on the boundary of the psychic and the somatic, of inside and outside.

Within the psychic context, the problem of boundaries also arises in connection with the agencies as endopsychic systems. For example, if the ego ideals, regarded as substitutive formations for the first narcissistic perfection, are held to take over from primary narcissism, they will always be 'a substitute from which the ego is separated by a gap, a rent that man is constantly seeking to abolish' (Chasseguet-Smirgel, 1985, p. 5).[23] As for the superego, the heir to the Oedipus complex, Freud sees it as linked with both the ego and the ego ideal; but it is also distinguished from them by its function of prohibiting erotic or aggressive libidinal manifestations and by the way it is conceptualized in the second theory of the drives.

The problems arising here therefore concern the separation, or even (perhaps only relative) compartmentalization or, conversely, decompartmentalization, of the various endopsychic formations, depending on the movements of cathexis/countercathexis and decathexis/recathexis that occur.

Work with borderline patients has shown that the ego ideal predominates over the superego in the clinical manifestations, whereas the opposite is found to be the case in so-called normal development. The ego ideal here remains close to the ideal ego, the mirror of maternal omnipotence, an airtight space in which nothing is impossible. Meanwhile, the superego remains tributary to an ego obliged to seek the favour of external objects.

The upshot of the foregoing is that the differentiations in the ego dimensions that we call ego ideals and superego lack stability and clarity. I therefore discuss these matters here mainly in terms of ego problems, although I do, of course, take account of the constellations which emerge or stand out in the organization of the ego.

In the first topography, the preconscious–conscious system is established on the basis of cathexes, whose stability ensures adequate binding and the meaningful use of representations. Borderline patients show many signs of deficient intersystemic delimitation: for instance, representations steeped in thought-disturbing fantasy elements; the manner in which the world and the self are perceived;[24] repeated breaches and failures of binding; the tendency for sudden discharges of excitation; and abrupt decathexes.

It should be noted here that, since the necessity to cathect is drive-related, the relevant problem in borderline states has a number of aspects, including in particular the fusion and defusion of the two drive currents; I shall return to this point later.

However, a few matters remain to be clarified. The problem in borderline states is not that the boundaries are uncathected, but that the cathexes are precarious. Failures of libidinal binding result from the fact that the perception of lines of separation immediately introduces the representation of a barrier that prevents contact, but these lines may also become an area of transition towards 'the other', outside oneself and in oneself. This representation thus introduces the element of difference into an organization which survives mainly by its references to the 'same'. The waves of separation anxiety – or, conversely, intrusion anxiety – aroused by this representation serve to mask what is actually a delimitation anxiety. After all, either the representation of boundaries is decathected, in which case what takes the stage are fantasies of primary identification or projective identification, or the cathexis is maintained; but in the latter case the 'unlimited' is lost and differences between what stays on one side and what is accommodated in the 'other' are introduced. Because it is dominated by infantile megalomania and the pressure of the drives, the ego cannot accept this, so that it is then at risk either of terrifying intrusions or of total exclusion of objects.[25] In this case, as Winnicott says (1971, p. 110), annihilation means 'no hope'. To be more specific, I would say 'no hope of finding itself again'.

The deployment of mechanisms of splitting or projection is actually a way of protecting against the diffuse and almost constant anxiety of delimitation, which underlies both separation and intrusion anxieties. It is an anxiety which stems just as much from the uncertainty of limits as from the wish to destroy them.

The ego in its relations with the object

When A. Green in 1983 raised the question of the status of object and subject in the constitution of the human individual, he pointed out that each object refers to something quite different from itself, something that is not the subject either. He referred to the 'other of the object', thereby presupposing a fundamental ternary structure made up of the subject, the object and the other of the object. However, what happens when the object refers mainly to the 'same' of the subject, as we find in many narcissistic and borderline structures?

Concerning the constitution of the not me and of the object, as opposed to the stage of a substantially undifferentiated self-sensoriality and self-sensuality, in my opinion account must be taken of the action, from the very beginning of life, of the various experiences that stem at one and the same time from the subject's own body and from that of the mother. We must also consider the subject's psychic work on the memory traces of elementary experiences, whether satisfying or otherwise.[26] The recathexis of the traces of experiences of satisfaction seems to me to be the first sign of the working of a psychic apparatus attempting to find its place in a world without limits. This work is facilitated, firstly, by the mother's activities (reverie and alternation of presences and absences), which encourage the development of the sense of continuity and of psychic cohesion, and, secondly, by the twofold trends of narcissism and antinarcissism, as defined by F. Pasche (1969, p. 227). The complex processes of internalization and externalization described by Freud, Abraham, Ferenczi, Melanie Klein and others,[27] extending from fantasies of incorporation to secondary identifications, reveal the object as both constitutive of and constituted by the ego, while the same is true of the ego in relation to the object.

However, what is the situation when the object is not the result of psychic interactions or movements which show the experience to be different from, although bearing the stamp of, the fantasy? Plainly, the object and its constitution are multifaceted, and cannot be considered in isolation from the fate of drive cathexes.[28] Whereas, from the psycho-analytic viewpoint, not only the internal object but also to a great extent the external object is fundamentally the result of a $\pi o \acute{\iota} \eta o \iota \varsigma$ (making) by the binding cathexes of libido − the object being what absorbs the erotic or aggressive cathexes directed towards 'the other' within or outside the psychic apparatus − the situation is clearly very different in the case of narcissistic objects. This is mainly because the cathexes are directed primarily towards the ego, of which the object is largely nothing but the reflection or double (although its characteristics may vary subtly or otherwise over a period of time). In the optimum case, where the pathology of narcissism allows the defensive narcissistic armour to be kept tightly closed, so that ego cohesion remains intact, heterosexual or homosexual object relations, seemingly with a powerful Oedipal tinge, may be established. However, these are relations which the subject maintains with aspects of himself, masked by a semblance of relationship and by its sexual dimensions.

This can be illustrated by two dreams of a 40-year-old male patient, whose narcissistic organization had remained unaffected by his first analysis, which had lasted five years. In his second analysis, with myself, the torrents of aggression and erotism unleashed in the transference had the purpose of keeping his narcissistic armour untouchable. He would not hear anything of his mirror relations and his relationship with himself, until one day when, through the similarity in the sound of the words for 'to kiss' and 'to guard' in his mother tongue (Φιλάω and Φυλάω, respectively), I was able to demonstrate to him the latent content of a dream in which a woman was kissing his ears, a dream which he interpreted as expressing his sexual desire towards me. What the dream was really about was 'guarding' his ears – i.e., 'setting a guard' on the opening through which he received my words.

Next day, the patient brought me a nightmare in which he was making love to a wild, half-human, half-animal woman, by inserting his penis into her mouth. The oral sexual dimension of his relationship with me was obvious, as was the terror it inspired in him. However, the most important result of this dream was that it enabled me to connect the wild woman/ animal with what he had once told me about the wildness of his own drives. In fact, therefore, he was also making love to an aspect of himself, while stopping up the mouth of the part of him represented in the dream by the bestial woman.

My interpretation led him to talk to me about his wife, who complained that he never spoke during sexual intercourse.

> I keep mum, I pull up the drawbridge. I never told you that, when I am having sex, the person I am with disappears. She is no longer there for me. In the end, I am making love to my own fantasies . . . I am ashamed; everything goes fuzzy. [He was silent for a moment.] *I* am that fuzzy, blurred thing. Who am I?
> Could my narcissistic armour be a protection against a void inside me?

A second problem is that the excessive clinging of these patients to persons outside themselves – which is both a cause and a result of the non-development of autonomy – is connected with the terror that the object might prove capable of engaging their feelings and emotions. They are terrified of being penetrated by the idea that the other might assume for them a value that would call their self-sufficiency into question. When psychic or external reality compels them to acknowledge that the object has assumed an importance that disavowal can no longer mask, hate and rage ensue. As one male patient said: 'I hate you, you and everything that might put an end to my religion. My personal religion is not to need anyone.' Another patient spoke of very close, adhesive relationships, in which he tried to 'get hold of the mind' of the other. He added: 'When I have what I need, the other ceases to exist for me.' Other patients have the feeling of being held captive in a suit of armour, in a trap, in a toothed vagina or anus, which hems them in and prevents them from moving.

At any rate, especially in subjects with impaired psychic organization, the object, when available, drains the cathexes of the ego. Its very presence is tantamount to a leaking away of libido from this agency, and for this reason alone it constitutes a permanent danger. After all, should the object go away or be lost, the ego would thereby lose a high proportion of its cathexes; and quite apart from the object loss, the ego would feel diminished in its inner thickness and continuity whenever cathexes were directed towards 'the other', inside or outside. The narcissistic haemorrhage of libido is reflected in the sense of a depressive void. This situation can reach an extreme pitch, as it did with one of my patients, who was forced by the slightest external stimulation (any visual, aural or other perception that attracted his attention or interest) to stop any other activity in which he was engaged. Otherwise he felt that all his energy was running away and that he was being drained; as he put it: 'It all trickles away.' He said that there was a breach in the continuity of his actions and thoughts.

This has nothing to do with depression, which is the result of the conflict between drive demands and the imperatives of the superego. Here, it is object cathexes which are experienced as gnawing at the self, as if demands from outside were eroding the energy capital of the ego. One patient imagined winning millions in the lottery and thought he would have to share the money with the members of his family. 'But', he said, 'sharing is like tearing into pieces. Anything that comes out of me becomes unfamiliar and arouses anxiety.' At this point he felt as if he were going to have a heart attack or to suffocate.

As for the demands of the cathexes of internal objects as images distinct from those of the self, these confront the subject with all the difficulties of preserving the integrity of his limits and, in addition, of maintaining contradictory images and identifications. The solution is often found in phases of narcissistic withdrawal, sometimes even involving the sudden, massive decathexis of object and self alike.

Conversely, patients may give way to fantasies of fusion, which are another form of smashing the relationship; here the second drive current is implicated. In these patients,[29] aspects of a process resembling primary identification may be discerned. It consists of recurrent psychic movements in which the distinction between me and not me is obliterated and the boundaries of the ego appear to dissolve.

These phases coincide with 'significant' moments of the analysis, in which intense and massive cathexes of the analyst in the transference relationship turn him into a dangerous object. The presence of the analyst imposes a heavy burden on the patient owing to the disclosure of desires and the frustration of their enactment. These phases also occur when patients feel the need to give up their habitual forms of reaction; powerful therapeutic resistances then arise.

These analysands react at such times by activating fantasies of fusion which ultimately pervade the organization of the ego and its image. This results in a total collapse of the reality sense in representations of the object and of the ego. These fantasies give rise to a feeling of sinking into the earth, of being swallowed up, and of disintegration of the limits of body and ego. The experience carries with it a sense of wavering and insubstantiality, as well as the desire to avoid all external stimulation – to 'return to the silence of non-communication', as one patient put it. In that desire, such subjects resemble others whom I have described elsewhere,[30] in a paper that discussed three female patients with a range of manifestations including hysterical symptoms, obsessional tendencies and borderline characteristics. These three women appeared to reflect a primitive mode of functioning of an ego which had separated from a part of itself, which it projected into the outside world and experienced as hostile. Once such a separation has taken place, the ego will coincide with pleasure and the outside world with unpleasure.

Although castration experiences were put forward from the outset (inability to express themselves, to cope with situations, to find solutions and to tackle problems of relationship), they were opposed by powerful phallic claims. However, more serious difficulties were evident in the background. The three women described themselves as being incapable of maintaining bonds of friendship or love. Their boyfriends, lovers, husbands, etc., could not endure their incessant criticisms and constant projections. Since their youth, the joy of loving relationships had been missing from their lives.

The hysterical side of their personalities was revealed by the exhibitionistic aspect of their presentation and by their oral greed. The anal components were manifested powerfully in their need to exercise control, especially over the analytic situation, and the obsessional outpouring of their thought and words, which put one in mind of diarrhoea or, conversely, of constipation. The borderline characteristics took the form of shallow, unstable affects, inability to bear frustrations and a need for immediate discharge of tensions, in the crude form of fantasies. These women also showed behavioural disorders.

With the approach of the holidays, at a time when the transference situation was characterized by intense representations of erotic and death wishes, one of these patients said to me:

> Do not speak. . . . Don't say a word. I know your thoughts, because I feel that I am in you and that you are in me. . . . We are one. . . . That makes anything possible. Nothing worries me, not even your death, or mine. I don't care any more, because you are in me and I am in you. Silence to the logos. . . . Nothing can move, nothing can go out. There is no more fear, no more pain. Everything is pervaded, invaded, diluted. . . . Huge waves are breaking, fading away behind me, in the whiteness of the ocean.

I said: 'Behind you, where I am sitting.' In the next session the patient remained silent, but towards the end she exclaimed: 'There are no thoughts, no images at all. We have ceased to exist.'

Again I intervened: 'We are here, you and I.' The patient began to cry, and answered: 'Yes, and that is horrible.' She was calmer in the following session. She told me that, the day before, on leaving me, she had suddenly thought: 'These tears, they are mine.'

Another patient, after a phase of deep regression, also spoke of her feeling of having been invaded. 'It is the inside and the outside, what is mine and what is yours, that is the cause of the confusion . . . as if I had just enough time to snatch a few pieces of my parents. . . . Perhaps I am attached to these pieces, and I can hardly see any way of separating from them.' She added: 'Now I am able to think about it . . . before, I could only feel it.'

A male patient announced one day that he felt that he was in the process of dissolving inside me.

During such phases of primary identification, all images of self and other seem to be blotted out, obliterated, while non-differentiation is a state both sought after and subject to the repetition compulsion; to that extent, I consider that this psychic movement is not only defensive but also betokens a process of unbinding, during which all the relational functions of the ego are decathected.

From the standpoint of defence, the omnipotent fantasy of primary identification eliminates the possibility of a relationship with the object, and can be associated with castration anxiety and unconscious guilt. Perfect union abolishes separation. Since it entails loss of self and other, it may be experienced unconsciously as equivalent to a murder, thus giving rise to unconscious guilt.

However, the same trend may be understood as confirming Freud's view that, as long as there is life, all manifestations of the death drive are held back and moderated by Eros. On the one hand, the defeat of the ego, unable to contain the anxiety and excitation occasioned by exchanges with the object, is reinforced by an unbinding tendency which operates against object relations, the system of representations and the binding of the affect; while, on the other, the situation preserves the very primitive link, by virtue of the fantasy element, which is already an attempt at binding.

Be that as it may, the most important point is surely that the repetition compulsion, coupled with a tendency to silence the body and the senses and to lose oneself by losing the object, affords the analyst information on the possible contribution to psychic life of the other drive current – i.e., the one that tends to reduce tension to the lowest possible level. In these cases, through the form assumed by the primary identification, the analyst may grasp by way of a representation what appears to the patient to be a manifestation of libidinal decathexis. At first, of course, only the analyst is in possession of this representation. However, it is possible for the analysand to gain access to it too, if the work of analysis continues – which is by no means certain with these patients, in whom the anxiety associated with loss of psychic boundaries goes hand in hand with the tendency for these boundaries to be obliterated.

The solutions of withdrawal from the object or succumbing to the primacy of fantasies of fusion are sometimes mediated by processes of adhesive identification or projective identification, allowing the occurrence of types of countercathexes in which separation is abolished as soon as it is introduced. 'You seemed icy when I came in,' said one female patient. 'You are an icy peak.' Later on in the session, she spoke about her feelings towards me. She was 'turned to ice' as far as I was concerned.

A profusion of scenes are staged in the transference: scenes of devouring; an image of the self as ivy growing round a tree trunk or climbing up a wall; a body resting on an 'anaclitic throne'; a slug winding itself round another slug; a hedgehog bumping into another hedgehog. These scenes bear the stamp both of sexuality and of a proximity which is either resolved by disappearance through incorporation, or seeks resolution in attempts which swing between the extremes of adhesive contact and isolation.

Yet these clinical pictures do not lack oedipal tinges. Far from it, as can be seen from the famous case of Sergei Konstantinovich Pankejeff and his relations with his objects. However, with the intervention of the third party or the appearance of the forbidden wish, the object is either idealized or sadistically rejected. At any rate, it remains unapproachable, wrapped in affective connotations connected not with guilt but, principally, with shame (e.g., 'he went away because I am worthless') or rejection. Borderlines thus cling to external objects – people, narcotics or prescribed drugs – or to frozen images which serve the purpose of countercathexis of delimitation anxiety, and they react with hate and destructive rage to what they may experience as distancing, rejection or abandonment.

Their 'being', in a state of alertness, defends itself with aggressive virulence (which is often concealed for fear of disrupting the relations of inclusion) imprisonment and immovability maintained with other people, or even with inanimate objects in the environment. Any movement or change is felt to be an exhausting expenditure of energy. However, when a separation or object loss looms, involving a diminution of narcissistic cathexes, some patients seek refuge in pathological forms of behaviour. For example, the subject may become bulimic, or he may stockpile objects he will never use, like one patient who bought large quantities of food which he kept for a while and then threw away, because he forgot it and would then find it had gone bad: 'It is fit only for the dustbin', he said. 'So I am left with nothing.'

The status of the object swings constantly between excessive presence and disappearance. What is no longer present does not arouse any wishful representations. Absence, which allows the neurotic to organize the fantasy of reunion on the level of hallucinatory wish fulfilment, is here experienced as a void, as loss of object and of self.[31] In other cases the patient may behave in such a way that his physical integrity is jeopardized through accidents or somatic illness.

A point that has in my opinion been neglected hitherto is that, in still other patients, countercathexes succeed in elevating certain internal structures to the status of an object, even when the object is no longer directly concerned, in the place of this lost object. These are cases in which a certain degree of representation, of both the good and the bad – the non-integration of which is mentioned precisely by Otto Kernberg – is possible, because neurotic adaptations constitute part of the picture.

A painful vacuum can be avoided by the countercathexis of an idea or feeling; this countercathexis blocks access to identification with the void induced by the decathexes or, as the case may be, with the decathecting object. I believe that the theme of hope, which I shall develop below, affords evidence of such a situation.

Countercathexes as the Guardian of Harbours and Roads

And you will be Guardian of Harbours and Roads (line 50) . . . on mountains (line 4), inland and island (lines 48–49)
(Callimachus, *Hymn III: To Artemis*)[32]

Any binding may serve as a countercathexis against the free flow of energy in the psychic apparatus, or against the irruption of traumatic excitations, provided that the energy can be maintained with relative stability and relative concentration on psychic morphemes or on external forms that take the place of whatever needs to be eliminated or modified in order to avoid disruption or disorganization.

This process is subject to the force exerted by drive thrusts and to the maintenance of adequate fusion of the two drive currents. It also depends on the ego's continued ability to repress, which is a concomitant of the satisfactory operation of the first objects as a protective shield against stimuli. It then becomes possible to set aside the omnipresence of the object and to modify the role of perception, which may severely impede displacements and condensations.

Finally, the process is affected by the manoeuvre of mobilizing energy around traumatic breaches, which give rise to excitations that the ego is unable to master.

Where narcissistic pathology predominates, countercathexes, fuelled primarily by narcissistic libido, make powerful demands in terms of energy concentration. However, they are not dense enough to yield a substantial fabric. As a result, either they cannot form the regulating screen whereby repression and ego homoeostasis could be preserved, or they nurture grim resistances which serve their purpose for a while but are not immune from storms. The psychic apparatus is unable to restrain and elaborate the clamorous productions of the unconscious when they emerge.

Freud (1920g, p. 35) defines the secondary processes as those required to bind the excitations from the primary processes. Failure of the bonds they establish gives rise, according to Freud, to a disorder resembling a traumatic neurosis. The dominance of the pleasure principle and of its modification, the reality principle, is not assured.

It is precisely the secondary processes that are impaired in borderlines, because substitutes are not readily accepted and the omnipresence of the object is not counteracted. Since the relationship of body to body, or being to being, leaves no place for the idea of separate presences, there is little potential for openness to effective representations having any degree of continuity. Perceptual stimuli are so intense that displacements of cathexes on to word presentations and ideas are not facilitated, while the anxiety resulting from uncertain boundaries limits the possibility of secondary-level transformations – for thought on this level can allow even the unpleasant aspect of distinctions and differentiations to be cathected. Here there is neither negation of plenitude nor obliteration of the subjective. The search for the identical is pursued stubbornly. The aim is to rediscover the same, if it is not possible to be 'one'. Even affects are not accepted, because they disturb narcissistic self-sufficiency and may entail the acknowledgement of differences. 'To love is to experience a loss', as one patient said.

Symbolic operations thus prove insufficient either for the maintenance of subject–object separation or for oscillation between movements of binding and unbinding, as well as in their rebinding potential.

However, it is not only the secondary processes that are inadequate in these cases. Freud wrote in 1920 that the gathering of energy around traumatic experiences was a large-scale manoeuvre aimed at forming a chain of countercathexes, but this cannot be accomplished effectively here. If it were possible, the excitations would be mastered. Now borderline subjects frequently prove not to be averse to excitations; indeed, they often unconsciously seek them out.

The narcissistic shield of coldness, indifference and rigidity, often adduced as a means of protecting the ego from the object, sometimes has the primary function of concealing the desire for excitations, which precludes solid countercathexes. It is therefore quite possible that what holds good in present-day physics is equally applicable to the psychic apparatus – i.e., that the relevant forces operate differently under far-from-equilibrium conditions.

To quote I. Prigogine and I. Stengers:[33]

> In thermodynamic terms, the basic problem has always been macroscopic stability, and the selection of relevant variables allowing this stability. . . . The second principle implies that the details of processes occurring simultaneously at each instant can be disregarded; it guarantees that any fluctuation that disturbs the equilibrium will die away. (p. 425) . . . A crucial concept here is the attractor. . . . A real pendulum, which gradually tends to become motionless, returns to its attractor state whatever the disturbance. (p. 11)
>
> However, in the far-from-equilibrium condition, other types of attractors may appear. (p. 12) These attractors do not correspond to a point, like the equilibrium state, or to a line, like the limiting cycle, but to a dense group of points. . . . They imply that the system they characterize will behave chaotically. . . . A slight variation may have disproportionate effects, causing the system to veer away from one state to another very different one. Because such variations are essentially inevitable, the system will therefore wander endlessly from state to state, exploring the whole of phase space – i.e., the space covered fractally by these possible attractor states – and its behaviour will resemble the turbulence regime of everyday life. (p. 13)
>
> Unlike dynamics, thermodynamics is selective. It aspires to represent the evolutionary mechanisms of a system only to the extent that they are meaningful – i.e., that they make it possible to predict the macroscopic regime which the system will adopt. Now the study of far-from-equilibrium systems shows us that this selection cannot take place once and for all, but depends on circumstances – that is, on the divergence from equilibrium, and hence on the intensity of the fluxes . . . fuelling the system. . . . We know the equilibrium state well. It is a state in which all processes cancel each other out. . . . However, we are also familiar with critical situations in which, conversely, the system becomes a true totality – not a harmonious and stable totality, but instead a literally unrepresentable state. (pp. 425–426)
>
> Long-distance correlations appear at the critical point. Any fluctuation then has consequences which propagate throughout the system. (pp. 17–18). It is the discovery of unstable dynamic systems that has placed physics at the crossroads . . .; (p. 19) the natural sciences henceforth describe a fragmented universe, rich in qualitative diversity and potential surprises . . . . (p. 36)

This, then, is the subject matter of physics today. The experience of clinical psychoanalysis likewise tends to bear out the thesis of an ego at the mercy of a number of different attractors, an ego that is just as prone and open to anxiety states and trauma as it is to homoeostatic and stabilizing tendencies.[34]

The primary and secondary repressed can thus be seen as attractors. Freud considered them to be opposed by countercathexes whereby the ego can re-establish an equilibrium state that enables it to steer a course between seething drives on the one hand and the demands of the outside world on the other. However, we are well aware today that this homoeostasis is by no means always possible.

Indeed, it is not even always aspired to, especially in cases where the unconscious attraction of situations of excitation constitutes a link – the last link – with the object that was its cause. As long as the wound is kept open, the trace of the object is not lost. The evidence for this is mental pain.[35] That is exactly what Catherine told me. In borderline patients the narcissistic shell, a defensive development of the ego, turns out to lack solidity, for two reasons. Firstly, ego-directed cathexes are not immune from the fate of cathexes of the object, which is itself in the process of ceasing to exist in its otherness; and, secondly, countercathexes cannot be applied to the outlines of the trauma, and hence to its delimitation. The attracting entity is the breach, the abyss of the traumatic, and, because of the dissipation of energy into this void, any cathexis is consciously experienced as both painful and always insufficient.

Freud used a metaphor in his early discussion of melancholia[36] that is in my view also relevant to my subject. He referred to the suction and pumping inwards of excitations, indicative of a haemorrhage of libido that affects and impoverishes all the functions of the psychic system. The feelings of helplessness and lack of self-esteem often mentioned in connection with borderline organizations owe much to such an economy and are not merely a concomitant of megalomanic ideals and the illusion of omnipotence.

Excitations cause the psychic system to veer towards an infinite number of possible attractors which operate in its space–time continuum and which inactivate defences such as repression and countercathexis. This is exactly what we observe in borderline organizations, in which the mechanisms of splitting, disavowal, projection and exclusion predominate.

There is also the element of the unrepresented, which exists in everyone on a level unorganized by language. The significance of the unrepresented increases in proportion to the incidence of obstacles to the linking of thing presentations and word presentations. Together with the representational void from which we all emerge, which is the common foundation of the psyche, this element constitutes an attractor in subjects who need to obliterate the boundaries established by the imposition of form.[37] In metapsychological terms, the attraction to the representational void depends on the relationship between agencies: the differentiated ego is attracted by a primary repression which it will always experience as a hole in its texture.

Clinical practice confronts us with psychic organizations that seem incapable of effectively cathecting the recognition and observation of their own psychic movements; the unknown in both self and other is experienced as a mouth that will suck up and absorb the subject. These difficulties can be attributed to early traumas, to inadequacies in the dams against the drives, or to narcissistic haemorrhage and inability to maintain a psychic container in which internalizations can take place. Ultimately, however, Freud's large-scale defensive manoeuvre of countercathexis fails to withstand the trauma. The reorganizations and rearrangements are unaffected by conflicts between reduction of tension and maintenance of a certain excitability in the form of desire. The psychic apparatus proves to be governed mainly by massive discharges, with evacuation in acts or in the soma. These discharges have their counterpart in the sense of a void in the subject's thought and in the negative hallucination of wish fulfilment.

Plainly, the preconscious and conscious systems do not receive sufficiently continuous high-level cathexes (powerful cathexes or hypercathexes). As Catherine's case shows, the obliteration and decathexis of the links between thoughts, as well as the repudiation (foreclosure) of certain representations, cannot but be facilitated on these levels.

Note, however, that the relationship with what has been lost (leaking away of object cathexes, draining or inadequacy of ego cathexes and also of the part of the ego differentiated into the superego) may remain masked for a long time by psychic structures connected with the ideal ego, the time and space of maternal omnipotence, in which nothing is impossible and no loss need be contemplated. The ego addresses itself to its ideal as a child would to the omnipotent parents. 'Give me all . . . , Papa', says Artemis to Zeus. And Zeus replies: 'Take, child, everything you want, and Father will give you other things even better.'[38]

However, the inevitable eventual disappointments, together with the inadequacy of identificatory internalizations, readily cause the coupling of the ego with its ideal to fail – particularly as the superego, with its dependence on megalomanic demands, does not succeed in assuming its organizing functions. The ego is then launched on a course which may follow different routes; it may find refuge in more than one harbour, or become fixated at many a crossroads. The issue will be decided by the strength of the attractors, which are closely modelled on the relations with the first objects and the success of their internalization – albeit in conjunction with the libidinal, erotic and aggressive bonds which the ego is able to mobilize.

This means that the ego may take the path of potentially psychotic regressions, or of somatic disorganization. It may also cling to an external reality whose objects and events are charged with reintrojected projections – a subjective and specular reality which the ego will do everything possible to control down to the smallest detail, because it is totally dependent on it. For this reason, any new element is something unexpected that must be rejected, so that it cannot be recorded in bonds whereby it could be integrated. The dread of change is here paralleled by panic at the unknown. It is preferable to seek shelter in the immobilization of thought and the unchangeability of repetitive cycles – to blot out rather than accept the sequences of displacements and transferences that call omnipotence into question.

For some patients, what must be protected at all costs is the feeling of euphoric plenitude, which nothing must touch, and it is all the more untreatable because it conceals anxieties about the void and psychic collapse. Some project plenitude on to the idealized object, whereas, for others, the harbour of self-idealization is there to protect the failing ego. The way the dynamic of hope serves the psychic economy is illustrated particularly by this last group of cases.

The last factor in this economy to be examined in connection with cathexes and countercathexes is the demand for fusion of drives.

Low-level fusion of drives

Freud states in his thirty-second lecture (1933a [1932], pp. 105 and 107) that every drive impulse consists of mixtures or alloys of the two drives (Eros and aggressiveness), albeit in varied ratios.[39] The erotic drives introduce the multiplicity of their sexual aims into the mixture, whereas the others admit only of mitigations or gradations in their monotonous trend. Freud considered self-destruction to be an expression of the death drive, which was present in every vital process. He thought that this hypothesis might one day allow research conducive to a better under-standing of pathological processes, as the mixtures could break down into their component parts, with severe effects on mental functioning. He noted in the *Outline* (1940a [1938], pp. 148–149) that the two basic drives, Eros and destruction, had the respective aims of '[establishing] ever greater unities and [preserving] them thus' and '[undoing] connections and so [destroying] things. [The two basic drives] operate against each other or combine with each other. . . . Modifications in the proportions of the fusion between the instincts [drives] have the most tangible results.' Freud discusses his examples in relation to sadism and masochism, but concludes that there can be no question of restricting one or other of the basic drives 'to one of the provinces of the mind. They must necessarily be met with everywhere.'

In a recent extensive study of examples of the alloying of drives in the various psychic processes and in the agencies, Benno Rosenberg took the view that the essence of the defusion of drives lay precisely in the polarization of cathexes involving the two classes of drives (libidinal and destructive), as this defusion reinforced the differentiation of and even the opposition between them (p. 568).[40] Withdrawal of one component or the other gives rise to tendencies towards defusion, which, according to their degree, may have positive or negative effects on the psychic apparatus.

In general, for the constitution of unity or binding – i.e., internal psychic cohesion and, for that matter, the cohesion of objects too – the libido must succeed in establishing and preserving unities, which the destructive drive must not tear apart. However, the death drive must also be able to establish internal differentiations or distinctions, as effects of a well-tempered defusion, in order for 'this concurrent and mutually opposing action' of the two basic drives to give 'rise to the whole variegation of the phenomena of life' (Freud, 1940a [1938], p. 149).

Unbinding phenomena, for example, when representations become detached from each other or from affects, as well as obstructions to free circulation between agencies, may be understood in terms of a drive activity in which the degree of alloying of the drives varies, so that scansion of the unbinding/rebinding movements becomes possible. However, if polarization is intensified, defusion is obviously no longer mitigated, and the whole of mental functioning resonates with the disunion of the drives.[41]

Concerning the effects of the defusion on libido, Rosenberg points out that, in this case, object and subject alike are ill-differentiated – as, for example, in psychosis – and that libidinal cathexis can only be an all-or-nothing affair. 'A good relationship between libido and its objects necessarily entails a contribution from the death drive',[42] which introduces the necessary distances and avoids collusions. I agree entirely with this position, particularly as I was able in a previous study of borderline states to distinguish between, on the one hand, the action of a defused libido massively cathecting objects and psychic morphemes and, on the other, the equally massive decathexes which cause the former cathexes to disappear as if they had never existed.[43] Concerning a different group of patients, Freud (1925h, p. 239) mentioned the withdrawal of libidinal components in psychotic negativism as an example of a process of decathexis.

Leaving aside the biologizing tendencies that inspired Freud's reference to construction and dissolution 'in the organism',[44] the 'dissolutions' are surely manifested at psychic level through processes of unbinding and decathexis. They are sustained by the 'gradations in their monotonous trend', which have to do with the scansion of the repetition compulsion.

The regressive movements brought about by the withdrawal of object cathexes, especially where narcissistic characteristics predominate in the object, are customarily alloyed with tendencies to decathect the subject's thought, functions, self and even body, resulting in the degradation of masochism and in somatizations.

Withdrawal of libido in borderline states and narcissistic pathology has been attributed to a variety of factors: separation anxiety; anxiety due to the close approach of another; anxiety at any threat to narcissistic plenitude; flight from the unpleasurable; avoidance of pain; identification with the decathecting mother; difficulties of relations with internalized object due to splitting of the ego; and so on. I myself would emphasize that the fact of libidinally cathecting what is outside and what is inside the self entails differentiation (because it is not just anything that is cathected) and delimitation, and that the inhomogeneity thereby introduced into the mind disturbs the economy of omnipotence. This explains why such patients reject change, just as they avoid choices (e.g., whether to be a man or a woman, as with the Wolf Man); nor can they accept psychic mobilization and the expenditure of energy involved in the cathexis of boundaries.

At any rate, the process of withdrawal of libido leads to low-level fusion of drives, as is also evident in the 'quality' of the decathexes. The type of decathexis observed in borderlines obliterates every trace of the prior cathexes. As one male patient put it:

> I know perfectly well that I was telling you two months ago about my passionate love for this young woman. But I simply cannot remember how that could have been. I can't even recall her face now. The whole thing is a complete void.

As every analyst knows, patients' experience of the void when there are no representations or feelings is painful.[45] This void, however, which is felt to encompass both thought and emotion, has two concomitants that point to drive defusion:

1 The feeling in the here and now that no alternation in the movements of decathexis and recathexis is possible, whereas in reality recathexes appear as suddenly and abruptly as decathexes.
2 The lack of any subtlety in these movements. The defused libidinal element manifests itself just as massively and violently towards others and towards the subject himself as do the destructive impulses.

During phases of decathexis, the voids are not negotiable. There is no capacity to assign meaning to them, or to bind them, for example, to a fantasy of castration and/or of the death of a significant person, at least in the most serious cases. At other times, binding is possible, especially in so-called narcissistic personalities, even if there are powerful resistances. For example, the same patient who told me about the void in his thought and speech (he could not think of certain words; he would lose the thread of his thoughts; and so on) was immediately able to grasp the implication of turning-back-on-himself in the words '*mon blanc*' ['my blank'] inscribed on a Mont-Blanc fountain-pen which he was given in a dream, and which we were able to connect with his relationship with me and with his father. When he was small, his father had given him a fountain-pen, which the boy had immediately lost.

I therefore consider that borderline patients exhibit temporary but repetitive failures in the binding systems because they cannot maintain constancy in the alternations of cathexes, decathexes and recathexes when the psychic apparatus is invaded by disorganizing anxieties. Binding presupposes separations and differentiations which omnipotence would rather disregard, the use of substitutes being ruled out especially during difficult phases.

When a compromise is possible, the sense of the unfamiliar betrays the maintenance of a partial cathexis. 'Things and time are there, but they seem to get cut off, to lose their continuity and coherence', one female patient told me. 'Time no longer coincides with events; I cannot remember what a feeling corresponds to.' This situation ensued after sessions in which the patient claimed to have won an area of trust for herself in the analytic setting. Yet that is precisely what was intolerable: the existence within her of an area from which it was possible either to proceed further in trust or to mount rage-ridden attacks on the link she had forged with me (the latter made her feel relieved).

However, certain violent reactions concerning experiences of loss and void in relation to object and subject show that the drive conflict is always played out in the field of Eros. This was the case, for example, with the patient who told me of his wish to 'detach' other people from himself, 'like ripping out pieces of flesh'. But the obvious deficiencies in the links between the derivatives of the aggressive and libidinal drives betray a low-level fusion of drives. This encourages the development of intense aggression, thereby neutralizing the synthesis of opposing identifications and internalizations, and blocking the differentiation and modulation of affects.

The alternation of contradictory psychic states, or their constant splitting, demonstrate the ego's difficulty in integrating negative and positive identificatory introjections. Again, it is when the tendency towards psychic silence is combined with trends towards the draining of excitations and their reduction to zero level that the death drive seems to be making a serious attempt to put the life drives out of action. I demonstrated this in an earlier contribution,[46] in which I described how one of my patients was unable to contain the situation within the mental sphere during a negative therapeutic reaction. Part of the excitation attacked the body and was negotiated through surgery. From then on, the waves of the regressive current no longer encountered a barrier strong enough to withstand them – for example, in sadomasochism – so that erotogenic masochism was swept away and degraded by them.

I maintained that at this point the second drive current intervened in the ego's effort to exhaust the intolerable, unwanted excitation, to cut itself off from its flow, to evacuate it, to silence psychic activity and to destroy the analytic process.

In this patient's clinical constellation during the final stages of the negative therapeutic reaction, it was possible to discuss the contribution of the death drive in terms of: (a) failure of the networks of thought links, which had plainly been put out of action as regards both content and cathexis; (b) cessation of desire for the object (what Winnicott would call deactivation of the object relationship and A. Green deobjectification [*désobjectalisation*]); and (c) the tendency for even narcissistic libido to be silenced. Concerning this phase of his analysis, my patient later said: 'Everything that went on in my body did not interest me; nor was I interested in what was going on around me. What I wanted was to be left in silence.'

The urge to reduce excitation to zero had put me in mind of the Nirvana principle, which Freud connected with the death drive, although, as stated, as long as life persists, only alloys between the drives or moments of drive defusion are observed.

At this point a question that cannot be set aside arises. In *Beyond the Pleasure Principle* (1920g, pp. 55–56), Freud repeated that the dominant trend of psychic life – and perhaps of the nervous system in general – was the effort to reduce, keep constant or eliminate the internal tension due to excitations. He added that the recognition of this trend was one of the strongest reasons for believing in the existence of the death drive.

Freud's three possibilities – reducing, keeping constant or eliminating internal tension – differ in essence from each other. However, Freud seems to take no account of these differences in subsuming them all within the Nirvana principle. He says again in his contribution on masochism that the aim of the psychic apparatus is to reduce to zero the sums of excitation impinging on it, or at least to maintain them at as low a level as possible. Freud does not here refer explicitly to the idea of 'keeping constant'.

By taking account of these slight fluctuations in Freud's views, I believe that we can avoid combining under the term 'Nirvana principle' everything Freud decided to accommodate within it at a certain point in the development of his thought. After all, the effort to maintain energy at a constant level and not to increase tension,[47] and to immobilize or avoid any factor likely to introduce substantial variations in energy, is not the same as reducing excitations to zero level, or to nothing, eliminating all tension and preventing any stimulation of the psychic constellation – a situation which Freud held to be the ideal of the psychic apparatus (Freud, 1915c, p. 120). At any rate, this ideal is thwarted by the demands of the libido. Furthermore, excitation is sometimes deliberately sought out in order to maintain constancy.

It is therefore as well to make a distinction. On the one hand, the psychic apparatus acts to prevent any increase in tension (whether pleasurable or unpleasurable) and to maintain the identical, which demands the draining off of any surplus excitation in order to 'keep constant . . . the "sum of excitation" . . . by disposing . . . of every sensible accretion' (Freud, 1950c [1895], pp. 153–154). Here I think that the principle of constancy is involved.

On the other hand, there remains in the Nirvana constellation the tendency to reduce excitation to nothing; cathexes tend towards zero as the system closes down into psychic silence and withdraws from internal and external reality, seen as an experience of psychic constancy and continuity.

One male patient told me that, at a certain stage of his analysis, he had felt 'inert in infinite space'. Everything had become strange and alien, and, 'as it moved away, it got lost. . . . Nothing can get near you at such times, and you cannot get near anything.' In his opinion, compared with this fall into nothingness, the terrible images he had brought in the early years of his treatment had been a relief. They had at least induced fear. This patient was presumably trying to describe to me something to do with the inertia of Nirvana, albeit enveloped in a fantasy of primary identification, a situation that was ultimately relatively non-libidinalized.

In another session, the same patient said that he closed himself to everything that came to him from me. He could not bear me to speak (my interpretations were experienced as intolerable intrusions), but he could also not stand my silence, which left him feeling alone. The solution was apathy and immobilization – on his part as well as on mine. 'Your death, perhaps? Mine definitely, as I have such a strong feeling of being drained.' The analyst appears in this sequence as the dangerous object that intrudes, sucks in and drains, and is exciting for that very reason. In terms of this discussion, the patient was thus trying to maintain constancy. In this case, immobilization may be essential in order to control what was intended to be evacuated escape: perhaps death wishes relating to the other and the terror of retaliation, or a massive fixation to the object and the effort of primary capture. Conversely, the drive current in the previous sequence was pushing not merely towards immobilization but towards the annihilation of psychic life.

It may be argued that there is no need to invoke a primary destructive force, and that a deficiency of libido may afford a valid explanation. Another possibility would be that of a sexual drive which, in seeking total discharge, turns itself into pure excitation and ignores the need to maintain the structural integrity of the organism.[48] In this case, however, surely the sexual drive would prove to be contaminated by destructuring tendencies. Again, can the ferocious attacks on everything that constitutes a relational link or a link of thought in borderline states be due solely to libidinal deficiency?

Of course, it is ultimately a question of choice. I personally find it useful to retain the theoretical hypothesis of a distinction between the two classes of drives, if only to keep us alert to the possibility of a conflict between the drive that fuels desire and that which seeks to annihilate such manifestations in the psychic apparatus. Moreover, because we are concerned with psychic life and with thought, some alloying is always bound to be present. In practice, however, it is obviously not easy to distinguish between constancy and the inertia of Nirvana, particularly as the defensive aspect of such movements cannot fail to impress itself on the analyst, so that he may be disinclined to accept the idea of a principle which, being directly connected with the death drive, could never be discernible in the pure state in clinical psychoanalysis.

My reason for returning to this earlier text was that it seemed to me that the negative therapeutic reaction might constitute another line of approach to the problem of drive defusion. Freud, of course, associated it with the unconscious sense of guilt. However, the in-depth study of narcissistic resistances has shown it to have other dimensions too.

The importance of narcissistic resistances was pointed out as long ago as 1919 by K. Abraham.[49] H. Rosenfeld (1987, p. 86) refers to defensive organizations aimed at combating frustration, dependence, envy and passive desires. O. Kernberg *et al.* (1989, p. 193) also regard these resistances as defences against envy and dependence. Concerning the negative therapeutic reaction, these authors mention identification with a sadistic love object which makes the subject feel that he can be loved only if he is ill-treated or attacked; pain and love are so closely bound up with each other that the patient finds himself their prisoner (p. 195). He therefore resorts to repetitions, in which he provokes the other to attack and reject him.

Again concerning the negative therapeutic reaction, A. Green (1983, p. 184) describes how narcissistic patients sacrifice pleasure with the aim of gaining the analyst's respect, and how their cathexes become progressively rarefied; although this impoverishes these subjects, it makes them feel that they are the best and the purest, because of their renunciation (in which morality becomes autoerotic pleasure and pleasure itself is abolished).

H. Rosenfeld (1987, p. 87) notes that fantasies of omnipotence projected on to external objects or their introjects, such as a very primitively sadistic superego, afford protection from any relationship with the object, and even from any relationship with oneself which might include the various, often

52

opposing, tendencies in the subject. Bisexuality and love are admittedly disavowed. However, I believe there is also an element of reassurance here, as a portion of eroticized narcissism is still able to attach itself to internal structures that offer protection from the disunion of drives, which would otherwise reduce their mixing to a very low level and allow destruction to manifest itself much more freely.

The situation seems to be even more complicated in some cases, such as that previously described by me,[50] since the negative therapeutic reaction does not only derive its strength from the ego's need for punishment by the superego; nor is it solely dependent on the narcissistic dimension alloyed with masochism adduced by A. Green.[51] Here, the hard core of the negative therapeutic reaction combined resistances from different levels, ultimately affecting what was no longer able to organize itself as a resistance within the psychic apparatus. The ego resistance was accompanied by superego resistance and id resistance in the form of the repetition compulsion. The destructive activity became obvious when the subject turned the outwardly directed destructiveness against himself. This level of self-sadism was manifested in the relationship between the ego and the superego, and, in particular, in the delibidinalization and degradation of masochism, which led to somatizations. Finally, drive defusion was plainly revealed in the tendency to reduce excitations to zero.

The separation of the drives was therefore manifest on several levels here. Clinical practice today thus confronts us with negative therapeutic reactions which must be distinguished in accordance with the relevant factors, as determined by the structures concerned, if we are to understand the forces at work within them.

The same problem arises with regard to the repetition compulsion, whose operation within the psyche and in behaviour is particularly important in the economy of borderline states, as suggested earlier.[52] Here again, two types must be distinguished:

1 Repetitions which maintain the cathexis of memory traces of the experience of object loss. They preserve the link with the traumatic element and immobilize the ego by making it too weak to detach itself from it, while at the same time protecting the ego from the depletion entailed by the disappearance of the narcissistic object.
These repetitions sometimes reproduce a painful penetration of, or forcible entry into, the ego at the end of an episode of masochistic pleasure, but the pain is often experienced as a mark of the elect and is then borne unflinchingly. In this case, the repetitions reflect an intrepid struggle against any transformation.
2 Repetitions in which representational elements are excluded. Discharges in the soma or in automatic behaviour are split off from the mental aspect.

We can therefore no longer be satisfied with Freud's explanation of 1914:

> We may now ask what it is that he [the patient] repeats or acts out. The
> answer is that he repeats everything that has already made its way from
> the sources of the repressed into his manifest personality – his inhibitions
> and unserviceable attitudes and his pathological character-traits. . . . We
> must be prepared to find, therefore, that the patient yields to the
> compulsion to repeat, which now replaces the impulsion to remember.[53]

The repressed memory is acted out.

However, the second type of repetition has nothing to do with
repression. Splits and mechanisms of disavowal and projection make it
difficult for thoughts which may be attracted by the repressed to be
transferred to a latent state, or for memories to be reconstructed. The
dynamic unconscious is not greatly in evidence, and excitation is
discharged in acts and somatizations located well beyond the pleasure
principle.

Ultimately, these repetitions most certainly do not serve the purpose of a
reunion with the traumatic element, or of mastering it, but instead provide
a framework for a failing psyche. Within the broad spectrum of
manifestations of masochism, the above view of the repetition compulsion
proves valid especially where masochistic eroticization is muted.

Three main types of masochism are observed in borderline states. The
first includes the various patterns of sadomasochistic relations based on
pregenital fixations. Here, the presence of the other is essential; the couple
relationship is required just as much for the seeking of pleasure in pain as
because of the inability to organize the fantasy of the primal scene on any
other basis than powerful identifications with the frustrated/frustrating,[54]
wounding/wounded, executioner/victim, master/slave, or predator/prey.
A delicious terror is experienced in transfixing or being transfixed by the
person to whom the subject makes his overtures, and accounts are settled
with the fear of dependence by fixation to the sadistic aspect, or by
constant maintenance of a 'state of alert', or, finally, by complete
abandonment to the other.

Masochistic tendencies are commonly used by borderlines to support an
identity threatened with diffusion. The sense of existence goes hand in
hand with suffering and with the oppressive presence of the other. The
feeling of being threatened with oppression, run to earth, trapped, soiled
and humiliated, in a way strengthens the boundaries of the ego.

In the second type, the acting out of unconscious guilt, which involves
the resexualization of the superego, betokens a regressive process in which
what matters is the suffering of self-punishment, and not the person who
inflicts it. The impersonal character of circumstances and forces beyond the
control of man is often adduced, thus displacing the element of self-

punishment to the outside. However, is it always a matter of unconscious guilt, which concerns sexuality and forbidden wishes, and retaliation by the superego? It is certainly not only that, especially when narcissistic pathology is in the foreground. A. Green (1983, p. 182) distinguished between fantasies connected with the severity of the superego towards the masochistic ego, on the one hand, and fantasies due to the combination of masochism and narcissism, on the other. The latter have the consequence of the renunciation of satisfaction, which occurs when the ego feels itself to be in debt to its ideal of purity. The subject is punished, through the feeling of shame, for never fully succeeding in its quest for something that lies beyond pleasure/unpleasure. Pleasure has to be evacuated, but so does unpleasure, because pleasure can still be derived from unpleasure. The subject is punished for the infantile megalomania that urges him on to something beyond the human, and for the narcissistic pride concealed by the veils of loneliness and endurance; his destitution is the evidence of his triumphant liberation from every need. What he seeks is therefore invulnerability to the advances of the object, and to aspirations towards the world and its pleasures.

Yet renunciation cannot easily be traced back to the ideal of purity, the heir to infantile omnipotence. First of all, this ideal may be formed by the reversal into its opposite of a production of the ideal ego, which is the desire to partake of the magic of a parent figure whose pleasures are boundless in space and time. If suffering entails the idea of a life of crucifixion, this is because Christ, by affirming that joy is not necessary in order to live one's life on this earth, is also the mediator of a possible reunion with the lost paradise in the beyond. The unending chain of renunciations in these cases seems to prove that no renunciation can ever suffice given the unlimited nature of desires.

Secondly, it is not unusual in borderline organizations for the suffering due to the shame of never achieving ideal perfection to be connected with the sense of an inner deficiency, which the suffering tries to conceal and the shame accentuates. Shame is suffering for a part of the self that is always deficient relative to the sought after plenitude. What is not accepted when desire is relinquished is therefore incompletion, and it is this idea that impels the subject to renounce, in order to obliterate the signs that might betray the deficiency. It is a matter of an − ever-widening − circle of movements whereby the pleasures of this world are forsaken; and in this circle, when renunciation succeeds, the deadening of pain is the hallmark of the de-eroticization of masochism.

Even more telling examples of this situation are the self-destructive manifestations in which eroticized masochism is muted from the outset, if not completely neutralized. Discharges become divorced from representations. Destructiveness, which is very different from aggression directed outwards or turned back secondarily on the subject, indicates that the drives are mixed at such a low level that neither the subject's body, nor indeed his life, is any longer effectively protected from it.[55]

Of course, it is not always possible to distinguish between, firstly, the deeply buried pleasure of a grandiose self triumphing by destroying itself; secondly, the furious satisfaction of self-destruction in order to destroy the image of the envied object within oneself; and, thirdly, the self-destructive movements in which masochistic degradation tends to silence the libidinal element. However, these are situations in which the libido is disqualified and inactivated to a greater or lesser extent.

Depending on the formations and phases of their pathology, borderline patients may alternate between the different types of masochism, or selectively display aspects of a single type. Such an economy, or dynamic, cannot but disturb the strategy of cathexes and countercathexes. The low level of drive fusion, coupled with the haemorrhage of both object and narcissistic libido, impoverishes the entire psychic system, leaving it exposed to pared down and unstable processes of cathexis and counter-cathexis. The ego is forced to resort to mutilating defences, such as splitting, projection, exclusion or discharges in the soma or in behaviour. Binding capacities are exhausted, and the deadly aspect of unbinding and decathexis is often reinforced by a tendency towards extinction of energy.

The whole problem of the fusion of drives tellingly brings home the need to take account of the transformations of encounters with the external object and their fate. After all, if the object not only gives rise to fundamental conflicts similar to the subject's, but also functions without recognizing them, the mirror relationship that develops leaves practically no area free for the inscription of transformations. The full positive and negative implications of the analyst's masochism may emerge here.

Diagnosis and prognosis, and the progress of an analysis, therefore demand an evaluation in each case of the available energy, of the factors favouring or impeding its mobilization, of the routes followed by repetitions, and of the action of resistances. And hope is a particularly significant resistance in some patients.

Hope

Dynamic and economic aspects

Announcing to Ferenczi the breaking off of his relations with C. Jung, Freud said: 'I consider there is no hope of rectifying the errors. . . . The best way to guard against any bitterness is an attitude of expecting nothing at all, i.e. the worst. I recommend this to you.'[1] However, some years later, he wrote to his son Ernst: 'It is typically Jewish not to renounce anything and to replace what has been lost.'[2] This could be seen as a characteristic instance of the human tendency to oscillate between the reality principle, which demands renunciation of the hope that certain things might change, and the pleasure principle, which cancels out renunciation by affirming that it is always possible to rediscover or to replace what has been lost.

As the vehicle of a state of trusting expectation, or even conviction, that what is expected can or must come to pass, the feeling of hope is a psychic strategy. On the one hand, this strategy remains attached to reality testing, because it acknowledges when our hopes are but lures and illusions, whereas, on the other, it tends to short-circuit the reality principle, which, of course, hands down the verdict that our internal wishes do not necessarily correspond to what can be found in the external world. At any rate, by introducing fulfilment of the wish as probable and sometimes even as practically assured, our hopes keep alive in the mind the image of a good object to come, able and willing to respond to our demands.

D. Winnicott (1958, pp. 309–310) held that this good object corresponds to something possessed in the past, in the first relationship, and that the hope of rediscovering it may even explain certain antisocial acts, such as compulsive theft. The antisocial tendency develops out of the loss of something positive which once existed in the child's experience but was later withdrawn from him, resulting in the sense of deprivation. Winnicott notes two trends in the antisocial tendency: rediscovery of the object by seeking it even in places where it has never been, and provocation of the environment and destruction.

People steal at moments of hope, greedily attempting to make up the deficiency. The hope of rediscovering what has been lost underlies compulsive stealing.

The greater the drive defusion activated by deprivation, the more distinct the search for the object and destructiveness will become from each other. The degree of dissociation between them will then increase in the child. That is why Winnicott believed that disturbance of the environment by an antisocial act was a positive sign of an appeal, and of hope that the appeal would evoke a response somewhere. Finally, such an act promotes the union of libido and destructiveness.

In this context, the strategy of hope is used either as protection from a painful external or internal reality (e.g., an illness, excessive reactivated aggression, etc.), or as a means of remaining attached to what is felt to be in danger of becoming detached. In this sense, it falls within the group of defences against the possibility of a defusion of drives associated with decathexis of the object and/or of self. Recourse to the tactic of hope means that the link to the object and the narcissistic link are not severed and that relationship is preserved.

This certainly redounds to the benefit of omnipotence, because nothing is impossible in hope. Once helplessness and mourning have been circumvented, the desire for the object one hopes to rediscover offsets the threat of castration entailed by acknowledgement of the limits imposed by a tenuous reality, through the maintenance of hopeful waiting. After all, gratification would rob waiting, anticipation and hope of their meaning.

In this way, the superego is in a way outwitted, as nothing occurs which might activate the need for punishment. Guilt is circumvented – although not always. A compromise is accomplished whereby hope eternalizes the desire, which, however, is not fulfilled.

'What is the hope you lead me gently to?' says Menelaus to Helen (line 826) in the fourth episode of the *Helen* of Euripides. Again, as the Chorus says, should the desire happen to be fulfilled, it would be because the gods so will: 'Much that the gods achieve is surprise. What we look for does not come to pass' – but 'God finds a way for what none foresaw' (lines 1689–1691).[3]

Hopes fulfilled therefore fall within the purview of the unforeseen. Or should we say, of the miraculous? A miracle is 'precisely what is not foreseen', and a miracle foreseen is perhaps 'merely the representation that conceals the reality of death'.[4]

In 1963 Bion developed the idea of the preconception of the breast (p. 23), an early manifestation of the baby's expectation of the breast. The mating of preconception and realization brings into being the conception;

otherwise, anaclitic depression ensues. On the basis of Bion's ideas and of Piaget's experimental work, which shows that children adhere for a while to their vision of the world and deny the data of experience, H. Boris considers that hope develops from preconceptions of things and experiences 'as they ought to have been'[5] – for example, the idea that there must be a breast existing for the baby, not only as an object to satisfy the oral desire, but also as the hope of a thing it may have for itself, within itself, or may be offered by external forces. Hope thus becomes differentiated very early on from desire. In the field of genital sexuality, hope supplements the desire for satisfactions at least equal to those obtained by the parental couple.

To demonstrate the difference between desire and hope, H. Boris mentions the case of a female patient who deliberately remained overweight so as to avoid the possibility of seduction and of satisfying sexual relations. She was afraid that gratification might undermine her hopes of the experience as she imagined it.

According to this author, the feeling of hope, which often coexists with physical desire – our desires may after all be mediated by immense hopes – eventually becomes antithetical to it, especially when the preconception is too much at variance with what external reality can offer. However, the more specifically hope is attached to an object, the closer it remains to desire.

When hope outweighs desire, anything that is potential or lies in the future is likely to loom large compared with the present. In this case waiting, or delay, takes precedence over the immediate securing of pleasure. For example, a patient who literally treated books as if they were bodies to be devoured told me that, once he became able to work as a member of a group, he found that he could read a book 'extract by extract', in the hope that the others in the group would fill in the gaps in his knowledge and finish what he had left pending.

When a hope is given up, the result is not necessarily the despair, collapse or emaciation described by Spitz.[6] A burgeoning of desires may then ensue, manifested either in a demand for immediate discharge or in an openness to the possibility of fulfilment.

Bion is right to say (1961, p. 151) that hope tends to divert attention to some supposedly future event in a climate of waiting nurtured by the non-fulfilment of hopes. In this way guilt is avoided by the displacement which keeps fulfilment on the potential level and prevents its occurrence in the present. Hope persists as long as the state of hope remains. This state, or feeling, thus on the one hand protects the subject from disaster and non-satisfaction, while on the other hand indefinitely postponing, and thereby disappointing, the need for satisfaction, because waiting is inherent in the absence of what is desired.

All this, to my mind, leads to a conception of hope based on a stable image of the subject's self-esteem, which accepts the idea of the good that is to come and trusts in future possibilities and the relation to objects. However, hope may also rest on emanations of a grandiose self, which does its best to mask the ego's helplessness, weaknesses and danger of psychic collapse by an extreme idealization of 'oneself' as a 'chosen one' who can never be abandoned. This self-idealization is, of course, symmetrical with the idealization of the hoped-for object.

Hope has been connected in functional terms with the ego ideal.[7] It has also been seen as a project to unify the ego with its ideal,[8] in which case the absence of hope – i.e., despair – betokens the relative abandonment of this project. A depressed person no longer fantasizes the reunion of the ego and the ideal. Conversely, hypomanic tendencies are often manifested in an incurable optimism, in which hope is totally unrealistically preserved.

Writing in the Kleinian tradition, J. Begoin states that the first objects are invested with all the hopes of development and that the greatest suffering ensues when these are seen to fail in their function;[9] this situation is always experienced by the child in the form of guilt, owing to the infantile omnipotence that is the matrix of the depressive position: the child has been unable to arouse enough love and attention on the part of these objects. Begoin considers that the prototype of trauma lies concealed in a more or less secret nucleus of despair, related to parts of the self that have not been able to develop because the conditions were not good enough.

J. Chasseguet-Smirgel also emphasizes the role of objects.[10] In her opinion, objects have the function of supplying enough gratifications for the subject not to want to turn back, and enough frustrations for him not to want to stop at a particular stage. A child whose ego ideal retains the dimension of promise remains hopeful and can therefore cathect the future course of his development. Otherwise, each libidinal position attained is prohibited because of the loss-related anxiety that would result from its abandonment, and the fear of not finding a fully satisfying substitute in the next position. Freud found this to be so in the Wolf Man. J. Chasseguet-Smirgel holds that libidinal inertia can be regarded, at least partly, as associated with early deficiencies which prevented the child (the Wolf Man to be) from cathecting his development as such – a development in which the projection of the ego ideal 'ahead of itself' plays an important part.

And indeed, how can progress be possible if each new acquisition – which is always accompanied at least by partial loss of the object and of the previous mode of being, so that it entails mourning – does not compensate for what has had to be given up? What happens if the abandonment of passive anal satisfactions is not followed by the establishment of a form of anal activity involving control and pride after the introduction of sphincter training?

These important points need to be discussed in greater detail. After all, while narcissistic confirmation (B. Grunberger, 1979) is necessary for the child's progress – if it is inadequate, a cohesive ego cannot arise owing to lack of cathexis, in particular by the mother of the child as an individual entity – the following are equally true:

1 Exaggerated cathexis of the mother 'may result in *perverting* development. . . . In fact in this instance narcissistic confirmation is coupled with sexual seduction . . . [which] brings about the perverse fixation'.[11]
2 The subject's difficulties in cathecting boundaries – including also those between agencies – give rise to vacillations, which may result in failure to differentiate sufficiently between the ego and the ego ideal. The entire ego then remains steeped in the infantile megalomania that is normally channelled towards the ego ideal.
3 The same difficulties may lead to deep splits between the narcissistic and object-related currents, so that an excessive ego ideal may form in such cases.

Unlike psychotics, our narcissistic patients usually follow the last of these paths. Either these patients cathect idealized parental imagos experienced as omnipotent, with which they tend to identify, or the other exists only as a part of themselves, as a twin or mirror image. These objects are therefore necessary for the functioning of the self and of self-esteem.

If hopeful waiting does emerge mainly at a time when gratification is lacking, how are we to understand the persistence of hope instead of, for example, a depressive reaction due to the absence or loss of the gratifying objects? The answer may lie in the activation of omnipotence, which prevents contemplation of the possibility of loss of the narcissistic object in these cases.

A. Haynal wrote that despair is a feeling that the internal world is dilapidated, whereas the affect of depression is connected with the notion of change.[12] If anxiety is a danger signal, the depressive affect is the signal of a negative change (i.e., a change towards loss), and the fear of change is ultimately an anxiety about separation from states or objects. From this point of view, the depressive affect has signalled non-positive change – i.e., change in the direction of loss – with consequent mourning, which is not accepted in these cases; nor do we see guilt due to superego accusations, because, as stated, the superego has so to speak been outwitted.

One day . . .

In his description of the 'waiting syndrome', L. Altman draws attention to the two antithetical meanings of the concept of waiting.[13] The first is active: waiting in a state of alert, ready to act, after preparing the ground, while fully aware of the implications, observing and anticipating. In the second sense, action is suspended, and here inhibitions of thought are often involved. Deferment, postponement, taking another look, and not moving all appear in the foreground, while the intention to go forward seems to be lacking. This is what Altman's woman patient recognizes when she says:

> When I have to stop coming here I hope I'll be able to do something else besides wishing for my dreams to come true in the future. You get tired of waiting for the future but it's still so much more fun than having everything come to an end.

The situation resembles suspended animation, as exemplified by Sleeping Beauty myths: the subject here acknowledges that, for the moment, there is nothing to be done and it is necessary to wait.

One day I shall be grown up . . .

A male patient told me that when he was small, he had hoped that, by putting his mother in a barrel, he could prevent her from growing. When he himself one day grew up, he would be able to marry her, and he would keep his father imprisoned in the henhouse.

The deferred project, rooted in the helplessness of infantile impotence, may be said to spring from the same source as the 'absurd' belief in the penis that will 'get bigger all right', as Little Hans thought when he saw his sister's genitals. Yet this source also feeds infantile narcissism and fertilizes the soil of another reality, in which loss and absence are unknown.

In describing her fantasies of pregnancy, one patient told me of a repetitive dream in which she was sitting inside a room, looking through an open window and stretching out her hands. She thought that one day a bearded man would come and put a blue-eyed baby into her arms through the window. This dream condensed images of her own and her mother's bodies, and its analysis revealed elements of her infantile wishes and hopes: herself in her mother's womb, identified with the baby contained in it; herself hoping to receive a baby from her father, just as her mother had had her blue-eyed brother. The stretched-out hands connected the gesture of waiting and imploring with the idea of an erect penis, the coveted penis which the father and the brother possessed for the mother's pleasure. So she was not castrated. At the same time, the hopeful waiting caused her to avoid her anal problems and her guilt.

This dream is interesting because it allowed the patient not only to become aware of her oedipal desires and of her aggression towards her mother, but also to assign meaning to some games involving her own excrement which she had played in early infancy. She now understood why she always felt a prisoner in her parents' house, imagining that she could only escape 'in the fulness of time'. The same hope (certainty) kept her in analysis for years, in a state of waiting that took no account of time.

Another patient told me that the present had no meaning for him except as a reference to some future time, when he would have the knowledge and skill to make certain changes he deemed necessary in his personal life and career.

Freud writes in *The Future of an Illusion*:

Men cannot remain children for ever. [They must leave] the parental house where [they were] so warm and comfortable. They must in the end go out into 'hostile life'. We call this *'education to reality'*. They will have to admit to themselves [that they are not] the centre of creation, no longer the object of tender care on the part of a beneficent Providence. [. . .] infantilism is destined to be surmounted.[14]

Is it to be surmounted or, ideally, set aside?

Thrust into hostile life, Ulysses, the prototype of man wandering through the world, or man in a state of progression, had but one desire: to find his way back to his country, his native land, his space, the hearth and home that housed his father, his nurse, his old dog and the family he had founded. He had but one hope: that Athene, as the goddess concerned, would see fit to accede to his wishes.

It is indeed Athene who reminds Zeus that the daughter of Atlas 'detains the grieving, unhappy man, and ever with soft and flattering words she works to charm him to forget Ithaca; and yet Odysseus, straining to get sight of the very smoke uprising from his own country, longs to die' (*Odyssey*, Book I, lines 55–59).[15] N. Kazantzakis takes up this theme in his *Odysseas*:[16]

My Athene! Athene! Like eagles the gods clutch at my head to drown me.
Descend; do not forsake me. (p. 20)

I prostrate myself, I kiss your feet
. . . Save me, castaway of earth and seas that I am. (p. 21)

Alcinous, king of the Phaecians, is told by Ulysses (*Odyssey*, Book VII, lines 222–225): 'But you, when dawn tomorrow shows, see that you make speed to set unhappy me once more on my own land, even when I have much suffered; and let life leave me when I have once more seen [it].'

In order for his hopes to be fulfilled, Ulysses will have to turn away from the perilous enticements of Calypso, Circe and the Sirens. The Sirens promise him knowledge of everything that once occurred on earth and was doomed to vanish into the invisible, to be sung by them as they weave their spell. However, the result of overstepping the boundary of this lost knowledge is that, 'beyond the threshold, the lovely female countenance that allures and beckons you is a face of terror: the unspeakable'.[17]

> Then the queenly Circe spoke in words and addressed me:
> ' . . . and that man who unsuspecting approaches them, and listens to the Sirens singing, has no prospect of coming home and delighting his wife and little children as they stand about him in greeting . . . '.
>
> (*Odyssey*, Book XII, lines 36 and 40–43)

But surely that overstepping of the boundary is the secret hope, never to be overcome, terrifying, attractive and spellbinding, nurtured by every child of man. It is about partaking of something that took place long ago in the parental bedroom, before he was born; about the knowledge of what has for him vanished for ever into the invisible.

Kazantzakis's Ulysses is convinced that, since he is the hero of the *nostos* and endurance, his destiny is to win the battle against his enemies, the gods (p. 24), for he wonders: 'What does it mean that I should be deemed a human being? Within my entrails I harbour a god' (p. 20).

The child hopes . . . one day, with the strength implanted in him by his parents, *he* will become the strongest of the strong, the best of the best, the bravest of the brave. He may even hope for his encounter with a god, with paradise, and indeed with everything for which one may wait . . . until the span of his life on earth is past.

In *Waiting for Godot* (1952), Samuel Beckett's men preserve the hope of a coming that will be their salvation. Even after waiting so long in vain for this Godot, who exists because the boy said so and because his coming is hoped for, Vladimir announces towards the end of the play that they could always hang themselves from the willow tree, the place of waiting, tomorrow, unless Godot were to come, in which case they would be saved. Both D. Winnicott and B. Bettelheim have discussed the effects of an over-long waiting period, in excess of the subject's ability to postpone fulfilment.

Beyond a certain time, the object will – even if it eventually proves to be present – always stand for that which has disappeared. From then on, object loss and the absence of hope will be cathected.[18] Winnicott mentions the experience of a primitive separation agony that introduces the void and narcissistic disaster.

On the experience of enforced waiting, E. Bergler refers to the masochistic provocations arising from the reactivation of oral and anal masochistic wishes and to the risk of the development of compulsive repetition of passive experiences aimed at restoring wounded self-esteem through their active mastery.[19] It does not, however, seem to me that this aim can be successfully achieved, because the injunction 'You can't do it now, wait until you grow up' is likely to leave a precipitate of endless repetitions that cannot but lacerate the stuff of narcissism.

Beckett's *The End Game* (1957) actually presents us with the end of the game, the end of waiting and the end of hope. However, it is also the end of life. For nothing but sheer survival is to be found here, until the wheel turns full circle in the reminiscences of *Happy Days* (written in 1961).

It'll all be better tomorrow

> Sing your song, Winnie.
> No? Then pray.
> Pray your prayer, Winnie.
> Pray your old prayer, Winnie.
> > (S. Beckett, *Happy Days*)

'If I begin an analysis,' said the young man sitting opposite me:

> I shall not be talking to myself any more. . . . If only it were possible to stand being alone in the desert. But I need a voice . . . though I tremble at the idea of what you might say to me. Yet what you say will be the answer to my hope that my request has not been all for nothing.
> Is it a prayer I am offering you, because I don't feel able to listen by myself to what I have to say?

Civilization and its Discontents summarizes Freud's ideas on faith. He says that religious needs stem from the infant's helplessness and longing for the father. They are sustained by fear of a superior power, the subject's narcissism being projected on to the parents. 'I cannot think of any need in childhood as strong as the need for a father's protection' (Freud, 1930a [1929], p. 72).

The child must also believe that this protection will be forthcoming and accessible to him and that he is himself worthy to receive it. That is to say, guilt must not be excessive. Otherwise the situation will deteriorate, towards either submission and sadomasochistic exchanges, or the shouts of mindless rebellion.

The two sources of the sense of guilt, authority's demand for the renunciation of instinctual satisfactions, and the whims of a superego bent on punishment, come together to make the subject's history, during the course of which hope becomes the mark of the encounter with a father who agrees to afford protection and with a mother in the role of infallible gratifier. The hope is that of sharing in the fruits of such a meeting – as if it were possible to imagine some future coming together whereby the subject might acquaint himself with those elements of the human life cycle and of the sacred sphere that delimit the place of our exclusion, but at the same time guarantee our existence.

In his second Epistle to the Corinthians, Paul the Apostle says that faith and hope are the hypostasis (foundation) of the things of this world and afford dominion over the invisible. Apocalyptic thought is fuelled by the same mystico-oracular messages that tell of the hope of participation. We read in the prophecies of Deutero-Isaiah:[20]

> Say unto the cities of Judah, behold your God!

> He shall gather the lambs with his arm, and carry them in his bosom.

> He giveth power to the faint; and to them that have no might he increaseth strength.
> Even the youths shall faint and be weary.

> But they that wait upon the Lord shall renew their strength; they shall mount up with wings as eagles, they shall run, and not be weary; and they shall walk, and not faint.

> For I the Lord thy God will hold thy right hand, saying unto thee, Fear not; I will help thee.

> Fear thou not; for I am with thee.

> Behold my servant, whom I uphold; mine elect, in whom my soul delighteth; I have put my spirit upon him.

Here is N. Kazantzakis's version of John the Baptist's announcement of the coming of Christ, of the Paraclete (the one who is summoned by prayer), who gives rise to the same hope:

> Fight . . . , hope, my children.
> When the time comes, he will descend . . . . With his sword he will break down the final and most secret door of the Mysteries, and, trembling, you will enter the Holy of Holies.[21]

Much later, similar ideas can be found in the liturgy of Saint John Chrysostom:[22]

> Therefore, I pray to You, have mercy upon me and forgive my transgressions . . . and make me worthy without condemnation to partake of Your pure Mysteries for the forgiveness of sins and for life eternal. (p. 30)

> So that they may be to those who partake of them . . . fulfilment of the Kingdom of Heaven, in confidence before You, and not in judgement or condemnation. (p. 22)

We thank You, loving Master, benefactor of our souls, that on this day You have made us worthy . . . of Your Heavenly and immortal Mysteries. (p. 34)

When hope as a feeling gives rise to hope as a state, it usually activates those forces in the ego which make for process and integration. They exert a forward thrust, with a view to identifying possible solutions and mitigating psychic pain. The search for the Holy Grail; faith in an afterlife without suffering; invoking the power of therapy at times of particular helplessness – the quest takes many forms. Like the hope from which they stem, they serve as a counterphobic screen and guard against despair. However, our hopes seek above all to control the forces of self-destruction and dissolution. From this point of view, hope is a binding cathexis in the service of Eros – except that this cathexis may play the game of the tireless repetition compulsion, as observed in borderline states. In these cases, the course of the game is determined by the level of fusion or defusion of the two drives.[23]

In the context of hoping, the ego's potential will obviously differ according to whether the hopes concerned form part of an organized system maintained by the subject's own efforts, or whether external forces and other people are expected to bring about fulfilment. An intermediate path may also be possible, along which the response hoped for by the subject to his request is bound up with his questioning and searching activity, as indicated by the chorus of Sophocles's *Oedipus the King*:[24]

What is the sweet spoken word of God . . . ?

I am stretched on the rack of doubt, and terror and trembling hold my heart, O Delian Healer, and I worship full of fears for what doom you will bring to pass, new or renewed in the revolving years.
Speak to me, immortal voice, child of golden Hope.

(lines 151–158)

Conversely, the hope of Oedipus, behind his conscious desire to 'find', contains within itself his refusal to know: 'Where would a trace of this old crime be found?' (line 108).

The Christian proposition, of course, is of the second kind, as the words of the divine liturgies prove:

We entrust to You, loving Master, our whole life and hope. (p. 26)

Do not forsake us who hope in You . . .
For every good and perfect gift is from above, coming from You . . .
(p. 35)

Glory to You, O God, our hope, glory to You.[25]

As for our patients, they occupy different positions in the constellations of hope.

Psychoanalytic authors have long been interested in the mobilizing action of hope, when patients request therapy, when they embark on the treatment, and when they continue and persevere with it. As Freud noted:

> Our interest is most particularly engaged by the mental state of *expectation*, which puts in motion a number of mental forces that have the greatest influence on the onset and cure of physical diseases. *Fearful* expectation is certainly not without its effect on the result. It would be of importance to know with certainty whether it has as great a bearing as is supposed on falling ill. . . . The contrary state of mind, in which expectation is coloured by hope and faith, is an effective force with which we have to reckon.[26]

The relevant attitudes have to do with the patient's desire for cure and with his relationship with his therapist.

Both analysts and non-analysts have studied the effects of hope on various aspects of mental functioning,[27] such as the expression of emotions, somatic manifestations, the choice of action where a number of alternatives are available, and the decision to embark on and to persevere with therapy. According to an old study by N. Van Dyke,[28] the closer the correlation between discomfort and hope, the greater the probability that those concerned will accept treatment.

However, most authors emphasize two factors: firstly, the relationship between patient and therapist, which may either strengthen or weaken hope, and, secondly, the patient's personality, motivation and ability to commit himself, together with the origin of his hopes.

If all is well, is there any need to hope that things will be better tomorrow? Aeschylus saw hope as a refuge of the exiled; the chorus of suppliant maidens warns the King: 'Yet anger of Zeus The Suppliant remains, with whom is charmed by no pity'[29] – i.e., he is unmoved by the complaints of the sufferer (παθόντος). Exiled they are from a land they regarded as their own, which now seems remote and out of reach. Land of their fathers it may be, but it is also the mother's body, as well as a psychic space estranged from itself; theatre of a discourse of which they cannot take possession.

But one question remains. If it is true that 'it'll all be better tomorrow', does this mean that the taste for life will be rediscovered, in the hope of finding again the content that will coincide with the ideal, as in the case of the woman patient who told me: 'If it is lost, will you get it back?'? Or does the phrase betray a split, as in the case of Catherine, doomed to her hopeful waiting notwithstanding the gulf between her hopes of reality and the absence of any sustained effort to fill it? Or is it like a mini-brazier kept burning lest the glacial night of non-desire spread throughout the universe?

4

Hopeful waiting in borderline states

Raising of shields

If the role of hope in so-called neurotic structures is to sustain desire – to which it is often strongly linked – and to temper what is painful or causes suffering, can it be said to serve the same purposes in non-neurotic patients? More specifically, what is its function in borderline patients, for whom clinical psychoanalysis has shown to have particular attitudes to desire?

When the hysteric banishes his desire, he eventually rediscovers it outside himself, deposited in the other, who becomes for him the seducer. The narcissistic subject, however, retains his burning, conscious desire to be loved and to love, but comes up against his unconscious non-desire, which he finds in the rejection he projects into or organizes in the other. 'No one wants anything to do with me; people do not recognize me, in any sense of the word', said my patient. 'There is no answer.' Borderline patients alternate between desiring impulses and the absence of desire, between the affirmation of love for the object in terms reminiscent of those used by Dante Alighieri for Beatrice: 'O lady in whom all my hope takes strength' – and either fear of the object, because it attracts and absorbs the energy of cathexes, or the exclusion of any object of desire.

These patients seem unable to draw a clear line of demarcation between desire for the object and withdrawal of cathexes; between self-love on the one hand and self-destructiveness on the other; between totalizing narcissism (in André Green's term) and detotalizing narcissism; between fear of castration and the seeking of unconscious pleasure in its accomplishment.

Clinical work with borderline patients is characterized by oscillations covering the entire range of these contradictory tendencies, and shows the extent to which these patients need to remain uncommitted, uncertain about their choices. Hope, after all, takes strength in, and for, uncertainty.

70

Concerning the seeking out of castration, Freud wrote of the ego demanding the punishment of castration by the superego. In this case, resexualization of the relationship between agencies, which themselves of course came into being in consequence of a division of the once unified ego, becomes the governing factor of pleasure. The ego again forges a particular link with this separate part of itself, which is no longer subject to its control but instead controls it. In a way, the ego ultimately regains control of the situation in this form of masochism, and does not rest until it has succeeded in being crushed by the superego, punishment which it demands. In these patients, however, the difficulties are compounded on two levels. Firstly, masochism proves to be closely bound up with narcissism, which gives it a particular tinge. Secondly, as Freud noted in connection with the negative therapeutic reaction, there is a destructiveness which is not bound even at superego level. Destructiveness worms its way into the whole of the psychic apparatus. This is a fact of observation, as shown above in relation to the negative therapeutic reactions of patients with extremely fragile egos.[1] As Freud puts it:

> One portion of this force has been recognized by us, undoubtedly with justice, as the sense of guilt and need for punishment, and has been localized by us in the ego's relation to the super-ego. But this is only the portion of it which is, as it were, psychically bound by the super-ego and thus becomes recognizable; other quotas of the same force, whether bound or free, may be at work in other, unspecified places.[2]

This view is restated in the *Outline* (1940a [1938], p. 180). Again in the context of the negative therapeutic reaction, Freud mentions the need to be ill or to suffer, and the sense of guilt. He then adds:

> It is less easy to demonstrate the existence of another resistance, our means of combating which are specially inadequate. There are some neurotics in whom, to judge by all their reactions, the instinct of self-preservation has actually been reversed. They seem to aim at nothing other than self-injury and self-destruction. It is possible too that the people who in fact do in the end commit suicide belong to this group. It is to be assumed that in such people far-reaching defusions of instinct [drive] have taken place, as a result of which there has been a liberation of excessive quantities of the destructive instinct [drive] directed inwards.

Although Freud here uses his familiar term 'neurotic', he is, however, referring to situations of thoroughgoing defusion of drives, in which the predominance of self-destruction gives rise to unbinding and even to the break-up of structures in all psychic systems. This means that all psychic functions are disrupted and that their specifying characteristics are threatened. This is so with borderline patients, especially where events and/ or the risks of internal change disturb psychic homoeostasis. One patient, for example, said that he felt absolutely worn out and was afraid he was going to have a heart attack, so that he took to his bed for more than a month. This reaction followed certain initiatives: he had helped his mother with money, whereas *he* had hitherto always been in the hard-up position; and he himself had raised the issue of paying more for his sessions, whereas he had always thought that his analysis was ruining him – not only financially, but also in terms of his psychic and somatic resources, which he felt to be diminished.

Such a situation therefore calls for urgent action, particularly as decathexes ensue and efforts are made to reduce the level of excitations. At this point hope may ensconce itself; its position relative to desire is odd, but understandable in the context of these subjects' problems (it is neither here nor there; neither on this side nor on that – and therefore on both sides together – but at the same time it is nowhere, because the whole point is to avoid a commitment to one side).

Hope eventually replaces the pleasure of satisfaction and also, in effect, desire. It either becomes established as a relatively close or relatively remote link with the object, still tending to postpone fulfilment of the desire, or sets itself up as a cathexis in place of the object. In this case, the subject can continue to hope against hope, or to hope lest hope be lost, as my patient Catherine put it.

P. Pruyser writes that hope arises at times when self-love is diminished or when the ego is not powerfully cathected.[3] The ego does not then experience itself as the centre of actions and affects. It feels dispossessed of its strength and caught in the toils of calamity and despair, but, because it still does not want to relinquish the representation of its participation in life, it organizes a psychic activity open to the future.

As we have recently been reminded,[4] all waiting, and hence also hopeful waiting, necessarily disappears in narcissistic collapse. Except at such times, hope in my view need not be accompanied by a diminution of narcissism. I believe it emerges in different contexts according to its source. It may uphold highly cathected narcissistic ideals, or it may arise in situations when the ego is in danger of dissolution, or, conversely, in phases of narcissistic reorganization. It may spring from a relationship, or it may be a branch, a derivative of infantile helplessness, to which the subject clings when isolation becomes unbearable.

M. Khan[5] uses the terminology of Winnicott, who considered that a facilitating environment gives the infant the experience of omnipotence because it allows him to develop the creative aspect of his experiences. In this way the subject learns to play with illusion and to create it for himself. The feeling of hope probably develops from the baby's illusion that the source of the satisfaction of his needs lies within himself, since the object is no longer in question once satisfaction has taken place and since the infant in any case does not distinguish the self from the world of objects, and cannot therefore localize the provenance of the gratification.

In Kleinian language, this would be considered as internalization of a feeding breast; the feeling of hope, which fuels illusions, would be deemed to develop out of primary experiences not felt as the absence of an available breast. The development of hope does indeed presuppose that the greedy insatiability which prohibits waiting has not become established as a defence against an intolerable internal void. Hope is conditional upon the idea of a breast which it is possible to find, as opposed to non-breast, non-existence of breast, or destructive fragmentation of the other and of self.

In general, hope is sustained by representations interposed between loss of the object and its potential recovery, so that castration anxiety is evaded or overcome and the deficiency that is not tolerated is masked. In borderline pathology, hope is subservient to the aim of magic control over fate, within which narcissistic megalomanic omnipotence is deposited. One day I shall have . . . or I shall be . . . . The same applies when this omnipotence is assigned to the analyst. The object is neither lost nor annihilated, and narcissistic shipwreck is avoided. Mourning and separation are not contemplated, especially as the object concerned is a self-object. Nothing is ultimately ever renounced. In the end, therefore, waiting may be painful but psychic pain may become a bonus.

Hope, as a compensation developed to avoid the risk of encountering the limits of external or internal reality, may thus interminably prolong the time spent in waiting and in action directed towards fulfilment. Some people's whole lives may be spent 'in making waiting their delight without noticing that the passage of time is obliterating their very features. . . . In waiting for the moment when they will really be someone, they cease to be anyone at all.'[6] The lines of the portrait have become blurred.

A person may hope to change his fate and thus refuse to coincide with tragedy. It is also possible to wait hopefully for the melting away of boundaries, i.e., the boundaries that reveal to us what they delimit: the other both within and outside ourselves.

To wander at the whim of boundless hopes means not encountering delimitation anxiety, never having to confront the *heteron*; such subjects may even go on hoping never to cross the threshold of the radical otherness of death. This is perhaps how we should understand the transition from hope accompanied by aim-related representations to a hope without representations, which becomes an aim in itself, an enlivening hope that lights up the menacing darkness of the void and of psychic death.

A token of resistance

As stated earlier, the capacity to wait is associated in most psychoanalytic texts with internalization of the gratifying object and with the resulting self-image.[7] Conversely, impatience is a sign of inadequacies in the object and of a vulnerable and unstable self-image. The capacity to wait exists because there is a sense of continuity and because pleasure can be taken in the possibility of hallucinating what is desired.

O. Fenichel attributes intolerance of tension and the inability to wait to an ego that is too weak to confront the id.[8] Oral fixations – of which the prototype is being unable to wait to be fed – and early traumas lie at the root of insufficiencies of the ego, whose reality testing is also impaired.

E. Bergler considers that the aim itself is not the most important factor in the neurotic's impatience to achieve his aim instantly.[9] Impatience is a defence mechanism against the demands of the superego, which is in a hurry to submit its bill for guilt. Bergler stresses that oral, urethral and anal fixations give rise to different forms of impatience, and suggests possible equivalents between the inability to wait and the inability to decide. He mentions subjects in whom quick success, while satisfying exhibitionistic desires, is at the same time a disavowal of the loss of the breast.

Patients see any failure as evidence of lack of love, which activates their aggression and masochism. They then plunge into situations in which they meet with refusal, so that they can be aggressive without remorse.

In my view, impatience in analytic treatment often proves to be the result of a conflict between the need to make oneself autonomous ('to detach myself from you', as one patient told me – i.e., to flee from the relationship, to put an end to dependence) and the certainty that by not allowing oneself enough time, there is no risk of one's difficulties being resolved, so that they will surely 'return'. 'It is like a film I saw', one analysand told me.

> After the war, a young man returns to his village. He finds three young women, all of whom are in love with him. So as not to commit himself, he goes away again. One of the women laughs and tells the others: 'Don't worry. He'll be back in fifteen years.'

C. David mentions the case of a patient for whom immediate knowledge of what people thought of her and of whom she was dealing with, or of what she could expect from a plan or a situation, proved to be a way of finding out who she was, from the reactions she aroused and the way people looked at her:

> Hers was an indefatigable and pathetic quest for delimitation, stemming

from serious deficiencies and worrying anomalies in her identifications. One of its effects was to mobilize and channel an extremely demanding function of the ideal in her, a function that seemed to be exacerbated, even to the point of madness, at certain critical times in her life.[10]

The ability to wait therefore constitutes proof of the subject's capacity to endure deficiencies, to postpone satisfaction, and to mourn, while still expecting to bring plans to fruition, and also to profit from experiences by learning.[11] However accurate this conception, it seems to me to throw little or no light on two important aspects of 'waiting'.

Firstly, waiting is a situation endured. It therefore necessarily evokes passivity and/or passivation. Fantasy activity involving a greater or lesser degree of anal regression may cause waiting to be experienced as anal penetration and give it a masochistic tinge. E. Bergler is right that over-long waiting has a masochizing effect, especially if the waiting is enforced.[12] Vulnerable points in the personality are exposed and the narcissistic wound is reopened by the experience of being powerless to change the situation in view of the constraints of external or internal reality. Winnicott understood this well, as we can see from his description of waiting times that exceed the integration capacity of a baby's ego. Secondly, 'waiting' of course serves the purposes of mastery and also of resistances, especially if it leads to the repetition of passive experiences.

Hopeful waiting suspends all activity until such time as means for its resumption may become available. Again, displacement to the future allows the subject to experience the aggression aroused by current frustrations without guilt. 'In the end I am depriving only myself of satisfaction; I am not hurting anyone else.'

Resistance is motivated by two factors:

1 Changes in the ego and in the other are not tolerated, as they disturb the seeming impermeability of the narcissistic organization and its untouchability in space and time.

   The principle of constancy here appears in the guise of the search for permanence or immutability. Exchanges are feared because they signify 'yielding up the kingdom to the other'. The libidinal element is accepted in the organization subject to strict narcissistic defences which stipulate that, if something is done, it can be done only by the subject himself, for himself, in a fantasy of self-sufficiency that will not readily brook any breach.

2 There is a traumatic connection with the drive, as a result of which any drive-related impulse is experienced equally as an attractor and as a threat of inner agitation, or even of violent penetration, with the corollary of psychic mobilization, which must be neutralized. It therefore becomes necessary to annihilate the possibility of change.

75

This is the aim of the deficient internalizations which determine the pathology of the internal framework and the fragility of the container/contained relationship. The deficiencies are due to the violent projection and exclusion of anything experienced as a danger of intrusion from without. These movements jostle and become entwined with the surges of a capturing aggression, which arises at times of frustration or separation with a view to averting the imminent loss.

The resulting thought disturbances take the form of difficulties in the registration of perceptual data and deficiencies in the capacity for representation and symbolization. They encourage a concentration on loss and on the psychic void, against which the action of external objects often has no effect. Repetitions, which set aside the pleasure principle, are then inevitable, and develop in two ways:

1 Reactivation through the stereotyped repetition of the traumatic events; the trauma then appears as a fixed and unassimilated configuration. In analysis, the transference takes the same course.
2 Massive and sudden discharges unaccompanied by any fantasy, in which energy is drained off in behaviour or the soma. These repetitive discharges – counteracted by the life drives which are open to change – favour the tendency to reduce excitations to zero level. But their recurrence, in spite of the manifest defusion of drives in this organization, contains within itself, through the sometimes associated experience of pain and very primitive anxieties, the germ of a link between the two drives, if only at a very elementary level.

However, as pointed out several times, borderline pathology often oscillates in time, and also extends over a very wide range. The resistances follow the ripples in the current, so that their manifestations may appear in less extreme forms. For instance, the tendency towards psychic immobilization may be expressed in hopeful waiting for a past experience of pleasure, which inhibits action while giving free rein to fantasy activity. The aspirations developed under the aegis of fantasy conceal not only phobic avoidance of changes and of the new but also the urge to anal retention.

Hope and waiting are not identical. All the same, it is not unusual for them to coincide, and in this case I do not believe that waiting, 'as delay, respite, the possibility of postponement, can arise only out of acceptance of the provisionality of hope, which, as soon as it inspires us, we assiduously seek to satisfy'.[13] This would make hope an exact equivalent of desire seeking immediate satisfaction, but this is by no means always the case in the human mind.

In clinical work with borderline patients, waiting and hope overlap to form a constellation that represents a nucleus of resistance to change both inside and outside the treatment. By becoming the organizer of a kind of waiting which forbids itself to 'act' in the present, and instead cathects what is to come, which is seen as a reunion with an experience of pleasure, albeit transported into the future, hope has thus been infiltrated by repetition. Unpleasure becomes ensconced in the here and now, but remains open to repetitive encounters with the known. Meanwhile, nothing moves and the future does not include the unknown.

The anxiety of waiting and of the unforeseeable is relaxed, giving way to repetition, which offers unconscious reassurance, even if it proves frightening at conscious level, when the return of the repressed thereby expressed penetrates into consciousness. As Freud reminds us, in the class of things that frighten us by arousing uncanny feelings due to the return of the repressed, 'it must be a matter of indifference whether what is uncanny was itself originally frightening or whether it carried some *other* affect'.[14] The situation in fact definitely bears the stamp of affects involving the familiar, the known, that which has already been met with.

Hope in this case takes the place of transformations, of change and of the potential for psychic mobilization. At the expense of fulfilment in the present, and of finality, it keeps the possibility of the repetition of pleasure in the foreground. That is why Dante Alighieri inscribed upon the gates of Hell: 'Abandon every hope, all you who enter.'

Safeguarding masochism

The various manifestations of masochism, whether involving the body or confined to the psychic field, are the theatre of many intersecting drive and defensive currents, overlain by a huge diversity of fantasies and/or forms of acting out. Masochism is a multidetermined and multidetermining constellation in which somatic pain or psychic suffering is associated in different ways with pleasure; both as clinical experience and as a concept, it has been presented so as to highlight different facets, revealing the intertwining of drives, defences, character structures, object relations and the relation to the self.

Since Freud's pioneering contribution in 1924, there has been a plethora of psychoanalytic literature on masochism, focusing on aspects such as the problem of passivity/activity; the connection with sadism; defence against loss, separation and depressive anxieties; attachment to an external or internal love object which, although punitive, reassures the subject about non-separation; the role of the parental imagos; the role of identifications; and so on.

As long ago as in 1936,[15] psychoanalysts began to consider the effect of early experiences on the development of masochism. The investigation of these matters has continued to occupy the psychoanalytic community, and other authors have stressed the pain-mediated pleasure inherent in the feeling of creating an identity for oneself and even simply of existing – or, in the specific form mentioned by M. Khan,[16] of existing through the body when mental life is petrified and psychic suffering is obliterated. Perverse or moral masochism is then used as a way of feeling that one is alive.

M. de M'Uzan discusses the perverse masochist who experiences in his body what for others is no more than fantasy, and who submits to painful maltreatment not to obtain pleasure but in order to experience and recognize himself.[17] Pain is certainly involved in the triggering and especially in the violent upsurge of sexual excitation, but it is first and foremost the instrument of the process of individuation on the one hand, and, on the other, the element that increases the demand for the discharge of sexual tension, which rises to a higher pitch the more imperfectly the ego's redoubled efforts at delimitation achieve their aim.

Borderlines do not present organized sexual deviations, especially of the kind that presupposes constant and consistent object relations. Because internal and external object relations are unstable and the symptoms are polymorphous, these patients mainly display perverse sexual tendencies, which are themselves polymorphous. As O. Kernberg puts it (1975, p. 11), 'the more chaotic and multiple the perverse fantasies and actions . . . the more strongly is the presence of borderline personality organization to be considered'.

One of the most prominent features of borderline subjects is their high propensity to do themselves physical harm and to suffer pain.[18] This propensity may be regarded as serving the purpose of delimitation of the body and/or of the psyche, whose boundaries are constantly in danger of seeping away. The phases when Catherine, my patient, banged her head against doors or, later, struck her husband and was in turn struck by him, followed scenes of shouting, yelling and tears. At such times, Catherine said that she 'arrived' at an experience of confusional excitation; the blows to her body were her only means of 'palpating' her somatic reality and of recognizing herself.

In borderline organizations, the difficulties of internal and external delimitation already described are certainly concomitant with the low level of drive fusion, which does not facilitate either the making of stable bonds or the separations whereby definite boundaries could be established. Self-destructiveness is thus encouraged, as the boundaries between inside and outside are not sharply defined. The various expressions of masochism are more or less successful attempts to bind the destructiveness to the subject's libidinal potential, as the quantities of excitation involved are too great to be readily elaborated by these patients on other levels.

The forms of perversions which introduce crude and very primitive aggressive manifestations are the prerogative of the worst cases, especially when the masochism can no longer be seen as perversion and is virtually uneroticized.

In patients with better ego organization and more clearly defined intrapsychic structures, the reinforcement of masochistic tendencies is aimed at satisfying the pressures of a superego whose rage absorbs much of the destructive component. Any self-destructive gestures acted out in these cases are benign, and it is mainly moral masochism that prevails, bearing witness to unconscious guilt.

B. Rosenberg drew attention to the relations between guilt and masochism, showing that they are linked by self-sadism.[19] When sadism, the clinical representative of the death drive, increases, as well as the hatred for the object that lies smouldering beneath idealizing narcissistic cathexes, guilt transforms sadism into masochism. The punishment, whether inflicted by another or designed as self-punishment, is underlain by the masochistic desire.

The conscious suffering – not only psychic but sometimes also somatic – may be said to settle the account of the unconscious guilt, by serving as punishment. This is surely true, especially in cases of excessive guilt and of fear induced by the idea of omnipotent thought whereby all forbidden wishes – particularly death wishes – may be fulfilled. But then the feelings of destitution, incapability, passive endurance, inferiority, and so on,[20] which usually accompany psychic suffering as the conscious aspect of unconscious guilt, would have to be seen as tokens of the latter's eroticization. Guilt, when masochistically cathected, thus becomes a locus of unconscious pleasure.

This is where hope ensconces itself. In some borderline patients, 'hoping' means not only that they have opted for immobilization in waiting but also that they are avoiding the discharge of tension and remaining in a state of suffering that satisfies the unconscious sense of guilt.

One patient told of his hope that, with time, he would be able to grasp the difficulties created by his dependence needs:

> I tell myself that everything I am now enduring is a foundation for the future – that a tall, solid building will arise out of the ruins of today. That will be my revenge for the wretched life I am now leading. . . . Grasping . . . encircling . . . circumscribing . . .. What I am living through at present is the unlimitedness of my pain. Perhaps that is the price I have to pay for what I expect from the future.

My patient Catherine used to say: 'Because I have suffered so much, I am entitled to hope that it will not go on for ever. My hope is that what I get in return will be marvellous and will fulfil my wishes.' By directing the available energy on to hopeful waiting, the cathexes are applied to a reality which, being neither fixed nor settled, remains uncertain and pre-eminently undecidable. So the game can be continued without end or be postponed indefinitely.

Kierkegaard said that there was no despair without challenge.[21] Perhaps the same applies to hope, which, in these cases, belies the experience of suffering and makes it the guarantor of future change, meanwhile ensuring that the situation remains immutable. In the relations between suffering and hope in these patients, hopeful waiting is found to nurture and prolong suffering in the present. It thus belongs in a context of repetition, which plainly favours masochistic characteristics.

It is indeed true that nothing is done in the present to avoid suffering. Whereas it may be thought that 'hoping' mitigates pain through a fantasy activity which serves the purposes of defence, suffering definitely goes on in the present and solutions are put off to a later date. A temporal split is established, whereby pleasure is postponed until tomorrow in order for suffering to be preserved today. The hope that maintains this state of affairs by banking on the future and denying immediate satisfaction therefore becomes a shield of masochism.

However, the matter is even more complicated, for although devaluation, guilt and suffering give way to moral masochism, the experience of pain is not the main objective in these cases. The point is to experience suffering today in order to reap an ideal objective in the future. Masochism ultimately serves the narcissism of the ego.

A. Green (1983) discusses the vicissitudes of a masochism that subordinates itself to narcissism. He describes how the fantasy organization differs in the two cases: whereas the masochist dreams of being beaten, humiliated and attacked, narcissistic fantasies have to do with waiting for the extraordinary: being a person to whom exceptional things happen; being the chosen one, cherished by fate and the gods. Again, it is not unusual for narcissistic structures to mask the underlying borderline organization.

It is therefore understandable why the interpretation from the analyst cannot but be rejected in these cases, notwithstanding the incessant demands for it to be made, and the equally incessant complaints at the lack of a satisfying answer. The reason is not only that acceptance of the interpretation would have disturbed the subject's fantasies of narcissistic self-sufficiency and of having given birth to himself, but also that it comes from someone who, behind the mask of the patient's idealizations, is in fact deemed to be mere 'base human stuff'. When a person expects the Messiah, only to liquidate him if he comes so that the rebirth of messianic hopes can persist without end, as Bion (1961, p. 152) nicely put it, how can words which are by definition devalued be allowed to penetrate into the field of omnipotence?

The impoverishment of object relations, or even their abandonment when narcissism takes precedence over masochism (the latter, after all, preserves the link with the object through unpleasure and pain), is probably to be understood as taking place over a prolonged period. During the course of this process, the cathexis (by projection of omnipotence) of heroic, messianic or divine figures gradually replaces cathexes of human objects, metamorphosing them in accordance with the narcissistic ideal, but without complete loss of the taste of the relation to the object, even if the latter undergoes a desexualizing transposition and transformation.[22] The ultimate destination is, of course, the annihilation of all object relations. Guilt – which would then have very little to do with the pleasure/unpleasure polarity, as the end in view is destruction of the object – turns into masochism, so that the alloying of masochism and narcissism can temper invulnerability to the object and its decathexis.

As to the idea of being the best and purest, through renunciation of bodily drive-related pleasures, apart from the narcissistic libidinal satisfaction thus obtained, it seems to me that our earlier comments[23] must be supplemented by a reference to the unconscious level, on which no renunciation can be brooked.

Freud put the matter as follows:

> As people grow up [. . .], they cease to play, and they seem to give up the yield of pleasure which they gained from playing. But whoever understands the human mind knows that hardly anything is harder for a man than to give up a pleasure which he has once experienced. Actually, we can never give anything up; we only exchange one thing for another. What appears to be a renunciation is really the formation of a substitute or surrogate.[24]

Renunciation in the narcissistic patient could in fact be said not to occur without the glimmer of certain drive-related satisfactions that have different origins and belong to different registers. Renunciation should perhaps be conceived here as a compromise between two opposing tendencies, with the destruction of the object relationship being accomplished on one level but not completely on another. After all, if renunciation is in general so repugnant to human beings, it is even less to be countenanced in the field of the narcissistic economy. In borderline states, renunciation signifies acceptance of the idea that certain things can be abandoned, that what exists in one place and for a certain time may not exist at a different time and in a different place. The logic of non-choice, of the suspension of judgements, and of the non-acceptance of differences, makes renunciation impossible.

The entire relationship between borderline states and trauma perhaps calls for re-evaluation in the light of the foregoing. Whereas the powerful bond responsible for the repetition of traumatizing situations is certainly consolidated by masochism, and whereas 'keeping oneself open' can ensure that pleasure is experienced in the penetration of the ego by what wounds it, non-renunciation, which is in this case also the non-renunciation of pain, serves other purposes as well.

Firstly, the ego is reassured, because some link with the object through the wounding situation is not broken, even if at conscious level the relations of sadomasochistic dependence seem to weaken it. If a pain-prolonging object is awaited and hoped for, the hope tempers and mitigates the pain, masking the relations of hate between the ego and the object, and thereby also reassuring the ego's narcissism. Only the negative therapeutic reaction in analytic treatment brings these relations to light.

Finally, in a drive economy which constantly threatens cathexes with obliteration, psychic pain, coupled with hope, encircles the traumatic experience and thus performs a function of hypercathexis that keeps the psychic apparatus in a state of alert, or even alarm, and hence alive. The experience of suffering surrounding the rent in the stuff of the ego caused by the traumatic penetration confirms the persistence of cathexes, although they are always in danger of extinction. As Freud wrote in 1930: 'One may [. . .] hope to be freed from a part of one's sufferings by influencing the instinctual [drive] impulses. [. . .] The extreme form of this is brought about by killing off the instincts [drives].'[25]

The life drives are pitted against the death drive. The terror and fascination of the void are twofold: on the one hand the subject is drawn towards the depths of the traumatic breach and experiences concomitant horror, while on the other he tries to annihilate cathexes while shrinking from the resulting psychic death. Hopeful waiting constitutes a focal point within which the drives remain fused. The dead time of waiting is offset by the space full of hopes, in which masochism is safeguarded.

As Winnie says in *Happy Days*:

> And if for some strange reason no further pains are possible, why then just close the eyes [. . .] and wait for the day to come [. . .] when flesh melts [. . .] and the night of the moon has so many hundred hours. [. . .] It might be the eternal dark. [. . .] Black night without end.

This is what psychoanalysts would call the aphanisis of objects and of the self, when masochism becomes degraded and the libidinal element is disqualified in the psychic constellation.

A cathexis that becomes an object

Cathexes persist when they have meaning for the ego, which they have the task of endowing with a heritage and internal assets. Their function is to safeguard the wealth of the domain. When the cathexis of hope joins forces with a fantasy activity that does not become divorced from object libido, it is driven by a dynamic which seeks to bring together the ego ideal, projects and hope within an object-relations framework,[26] without sacrificing the relevant narcissistic cathexis.

To the extent that the hopes concern the object, they maintain the link with this idealized, unique object and with the parts of the self it represents. The hopes are therefore preserved as precious possessions. The features of the object which they adopt are there to guarantee that the trace of the object has not been drowned in the regressive current. Desire may still be said to water the psychic soil.

However, a closer examination is called for. This is firstly because the object of hope is an object enclosed within the ego. If it is able to merge with its ideal, this is because it forms a unity with the ego which allows the latter to do anything it likes with it in fantasy. The reality of the object, as well as that of the subject − insofar as the latter's present reality goes unrecognized or is defied − is virtually disregarded, and linear displacements occur in the direction of what is hoped for. In borderline patients, what is awaited and hoped for is ultimately the encounter with the same. Repetition plays a prominent part in the process.

Secondly, in the 'normal' course of development, if the ego nurtures its hopes as intimate possessions, preserved inside it just as Pandora detained hers in her jar, it generally contrives to give them free rein, as Prometheus did, for better or for worse. In other words, either the ego comes to an accommodation with external reality in order to fulfil its hopes, or they are abandoned after a lapse of time.

However, this is not the case in patients who turn their hopes into an omnipotent Pandoteira by disavowing whole areas of reality. Is this a matter of wishes for plenitude and the strength to fulfil them? Is it an antidepressive formation? Or a counterweight to the risk of being engulfed by the void when the aspiration to cathect objects and the inner world flags? At any rate, as a psychic morpheme originating from a grandiose self, hope in these subjects corresponds to an extreme idealization of themselves, which reflects the idea that they cannot be abandoned; this idealization is symmetrical with that of the hoped-for object.

Can we still connect this morpheme with the idea of unifying the ego with its ideal? If so − and this presupposes a good and sufficiently stable differentiation of intrapsychic formations (which cannot be taken for granted in borderline pathology) − we must deem the ego ideal concerned to be of inordinate dimensions, and that it does not come into being as a successor to or substitute for primary narcissism, with which it in fact remains so strongly impregnated that its transformations thereby suffer.

Hope, being close to the productions of the ideal ego, here captures the object, and buries and immobilizes it in a petrifying embrace, despite its seeming vigour. It places the object so to speak in psychic seclusion.

Hope falls short of the mastery and active control of the tensions induced by potential or actual loss situations, and of implosive or explosive murderous impulses, and in these cases duplicates a nuclear part of the subject moulded from infantile omnipotence. This part is kept encysted by the primary activity of a sphincter which closes tight without yet engaging in anal activity as such; it is a nucleus of the self immune to differences and distinctions, especially those between the sexes and the generations, and its fibres are intertwined with those of the incarcerated object.

The anal activity of retention/preservation and destruction/evacuation is often directed merely towards concealing the aim of primary anality[27] – i.e., that of total incorporation of or by the object – this aim being reversed into an affect of terror lest the object insinuate itself into the subject and take possession of its entire space. If anal power applies movements of incorporation/expulsion and rejection/recovery to objects, this treatment does not mean that the tendency towards fusion with the primary object has been given up once and for all. This tendency survives in the form of the wish to engulf the object in the self, while actual obliteration of boundaries is prevented by the propensity to initiate anal activity. However, this activity is unable to develop its full potential for the structuring and organization of the personality owing to the difficulties in cathecting discussed above.

How can the idea of encystment (in an anus-cum-vagina) be reconciled with the experience of anxieties about delimitation, void, deficiency, fading of internal objects or haemorrrhaging of the ego, so often observed in borderline states? The apparent contradiction is to my mind resolved if we consider, firstly, the persistence of infantile omnipotence due to major splits, which upholds the mental and affective suspension (neither yes nor no) and, secondly, the triggering of a primary capturing anality when a frustrating experience threatens.

Failures of omnipotence give rise to attempts to capture, to freeze and to petrify, involving the deployment of massive and heavy cathexes, which betray the action of defused libido. Psychic mobility, negotiations and exchanges are neutralized by the capturing retention. Furthermore, the attempts at object recovery which alternate with feelings of loss can ultimately stem only from dense, massive, albeit unstable points of cathexis, alternating with unbinding trends that reveal the defusion of drives. Massive libidinal cathexis occurs, untempered by adequate mixing with the second drive current.

In my view, the tendency towards decathexes, combined with the action of a defused libido that cathects massively but unstably, explains the swings between movements of loss and recovery, which also make for unwillingness to embrace firm positions.

In economic terms, hopes serve the subject well, as he then evades commitment to the object, but does not exist without the contribution of the narcissistic object. The object is immediately trapped in the toils of the capturing process and is removed – that is to say, it is relegated to a future which never becomes present. Yet it is held by a thread: the representation of a future reunion with it.

Narcissistic libido, as we know, does not privilege the object, but without the object it may well embrace nothing but the void. The borderline's oscillations between object loss and recovery are in fact swings between attempts at object restitution, engulfing seclusion, and destruction of the object.[28] These are observable when a person's mind 'goes blank' and in lapses of memory, failure to register perceptual data, and annihilation of traces, all of which demonstrate how far the object remains the complement or reflection of parts of the ego, lost without it.

Most authors have hitherto seen mental blanks, the sense of the void, obliteration of object traces and the fading away of sequences of events and feelings, as instances of defective internalization, due either to intrusion and separation anxieties or to the foreclosure of certain representations. The present study has emphasized the instability of cathexes, associated with the low level of fusion of the drives. The situation may be further clarified if it is recalled that psychically valid representations – i.e., ones which can become 'meaningful' in psychic life – can exist only if the psychic apparatus is capable of opposing immediate discharges and of enduring hyper-cathexes[29] – since the recathexis of memory traces allowing the formation of thing or word representations falls within the purview of hypercathexis.

However, because the interplay of cathexes, decathexes and recathexes is a problem in borderlines, the available representations are unable at times of excessive excitation to absorb and attenuate the sheer quantities that invade the psychic channels. Representations are either evacuated in a self-draining process, or are frozen so as to preserve substance in a psychic space felt to be in danger of emptying out; but their functioning in the psychic apparatus thereby loses the mobility afforded by binding and unbinding.

Again, splitting mechanisms prevent certain perceptual elements from being registered in such a way as to guarantee the possibility of thing or word presentations. Thought processes are in some cases barely cathected, as the fixation to the lost object keeps loss in the foreground and opposes substitutions. Discontinuities of thought therefore appear as permanent. Paraphrasing Luigi Pirandello, we could therefore say that the void must be clothed, provided that this is still possible.

Freud considered that, when the object is abandoned, the ego offers itself to the id as its only love object. But perhaps an intermediate stage should then be considered. It would be the prerogative of certain ego constellations, which are admittedly poorly organized in terms of their defensive capacities, and definitely lack the capacity to cathect their limits firmly and continuously, but which nevertheless do not allow conflicts to become located solely in the soma or in external reality. This stage might therefore be observable at times of relative integrity of a neurotic or perverse layer overlying a pathology involving limits.

In this situation an ego for a long time bolstered by hopes that afford glimpses of an – albeit narcissistic – object may eventually tire of and become disappointed by that object, which never satisfies by its presence in the here and now (although that is not what is ultimately desired). Held in a state of suspended reality, the object is sufficiently present to mask the gap left by its absence and to allow separation to be disavowed, but not present enough to obviate the risk of cathexis of its loss should hopes concerning it fade, in which case a repetitive cycle accompanied by narcissistic haemorrhage would ensue.

Another possible risk is, as stated, decathexis not only of the ego but also of the object, particularly if suffering is not eroticized in the ego–object conflict. Hatred of an object which merely feeds narcissism with wounds – that is, ultimately, hatred of oneself for having failed to inspire the ever hoped-for love in the other – may lead to a psychic reality in which suffering is not sustained by any pleasure and masochism is no longer protected.

When the ego is faced with psychic ruin of this kind, if it still has means of defending itself and a libidinal potential, it may be impelled to protect itself by abandoning the object and transferring all cathexes on to its own hoping. Cathexis of the process of hope replaces the object, and hope itself is cathected.

This hope is no longer the hope of something; it no longer knows its object. Patients go on hoping without knowing what they are hoping for. As one male patient put it:

> There are no more images . . . no more expected events to nail my hopes on. It is intolerable not to wait, but at the same time the unknown is unbearable. . . . Oddly enough, though, I feel as if I might have breaks or cuts in my skin . . . they could hurt me badly. But they don't. Mainly I feel wrapped up in my own state of hoping. Protected. I could not say what from. . . . Hoping for what? . . . I could not tell you that either. . . . Hoping is enough for me.

Is the feeling of hope as it were fetishized in this process? Or is there an element of affective perversion, which Christian David described as the seeking of pleasure not in the sexual act or in acting out, but purely in the psychoaffective register? Might the drive be aim-inhibited, with cathexis concentrated on forepleasure?

At the very heart of erotic desire, a gulf opens between the striving for somatic pleasure on the one hand and for psychic pleasure, derived from the workings of the affects, on the other. Affects and feelings are therefore organized so as to produce a pleasure confined to the psychic level. Affective perversion could be defined as a fetishism of internal tendencies, a fetishism without a fetish, and hence an inner fetishism.

Being closely bound up with moral masochism and longing, affective perversion selectively eroticizes mechanisms of displacement and virtualization, of both the aim and the objects of the sexual drive. The most intense reactions and affects are aroused by the virtual image of the internalized object of desire, and not by the object itself. 'On the one hand, therefore, the living strength of the drive is inhibited, while, on the other, it tends to become more intimate, as it drifts towards the agencies of internal perception.'[30]

My female patient's clinical picture lacked a fully conscious and deliberate search for pleasure based on intensified imagination, in which feeling takes precedence over thought, as well as the voluptuous modulation of affects, which is the main agent of pleasure in affective perversion. The compulsive seeking of impressions and emotions internalized to the utmost was also absent.

However, at this precise moment in Catherine's analysis, as also at other times of her life, when the pressure to cathect was intensified by the stimulations of external and internal perception, she may well have been tempted to show me an aspect of the defensive weaponry she was capable of deploying: the aspect that enabled her to see herself as the 'theatre director' who enacted her pleasure and 'to obtain and modulate it at will'.[31] All in all, she was presumably trying to protect the integrity of her person from the demands of internal and external reality, which she experienced as threatening intrusions.

While this view is possible, it calls for considerable qualification, as the patient lacked a dynamic constellation capable of sufficiently stable and coherent organization to govern object and intersystemic relations. I would not on that account wish to minimize the possible organizing value of such an essentially perverse trend – the outline of which I discern in the delight taken by the patient in contemplating the objects of desire from a distance – but I believe that the issue here was much more important.

The cathexis of the actual process of hoping – independently of the representations previously attached to it, which have been lost – in my view betokens an effort by the ego at binding, with the aim of allowing mental life to continue. For these are moments when the libido abandons the representations of the internal object, while the external object has already been torn away from it. There are no more expectations. With the onset of waiting without representations, everything escapes.

When cathexes are concentrated on an ego feeling or state instead of on the lost objects, however, the free flow of affects is halted. The door is therefore left open to the possibility of new associations with representations; in view of the mind's insatiable appetite for the assignment of form and for representability, this can take place quite quickly, especially during a psychoanalysis. A nucleus of warmth is maintained in a part of the mind that had been exposed to the risk of the frost of decathexes.[32] When cathexes are displaced on to the process of hoping itself, there is no discharge of tension. Representations are suspended, but in favour of an inner experience in which the ego does not fail completely.

The ego in borderline cases is rightly deemed to be constantly seeking replenishment from without and to be for ever unable to achieve completeness owing to the initial narcissistic breach. While this is perfectly correct, it is not so in every case or at every moment, particularly where the fundamental borderline structure is open to certain transformations including – primary anality apart – attempts at the mastery of painful situations.[33] In these cases the ego succeeds in maintaining an internal possession that requires less expenditure of energy than the demands of object relations. Self-cathexis then constitutes evidence that something 'good' is there to be cathected, so that the process of drive defusion and unbinding is discouraged.

With the masochism that it protects, 'hoping' thus constitutes a hearth in which the flame of the fused drives can continue to burn.

5

Even God needs a mother

Now there is no hope left for the
children's lives.
Now there is none.

(Chorus, lines 976–978)

. . . Many things the gods
Achieve beyond our judgement. What we
thought
Is not confirmed and what we thought
not god
Contrives. . . .

(Chorus, lines 1416–1418)
(Euripides, The Medea[1])

De-formation, de-shaping, dis-sociation

In a book about the different ways of thinking encountered by the analyst in present-day clinical practice, A. Green (1986, pp. 22–23) describes what he calls the logic of despair. In the patients concerned, as D. Winnicott had pointed out, the only possible reality is that which induces suffering by absence. Objects exist through the disappointments and unpleasure to which they give rise.

The mental life of these subjects is far removed from the pleasure principle, since the pursuit of unpleasure and the avoidance of pleasure hold sway in the psychic economy. They in effect say yes to unpleasure and no to pleasure, while the quality of the psychic pain makes it impossible to discover the nature of the satisfaction involved, even if it is obtained unconsciously.

This logic of despair is often found in severely depressed patients when the void left behind by the missing object becomes established. 'The angel of silence has flown over us!' writes A. Chekhov,[2] 'all my hopes are gone . . . no object in life.' The same logic exists in borderline states. One feels that thinking is unable to bring out the trace of an experience of pleasure, or that a good memory can be found only with great difficulty, and is immediately swamped by ideas of deficiency and of absence. Mental processes become disorganized under the pressure of feelings of hatred and destruction and the violence of despair. The subject seems set on a course towards death.

However, owing to splitting processes in the ego, the logic of despair often coexists with that of hope, which, as stated several times, is fuelled by attempts to preserve the link with the object, a link immersed in the ever-present memory of the trauma, when it is not obliterated by acting out or somatic symptoms.

In these cases, a situation of 'neither yes nor no' may therefore be said to prevail on the unconscious level, accompanied by an intense susceptibility to excitations, underlain by omnipotent fantasies. The latter surround hope with the fires of immortality and also steep it in an ideal of rebirth or self-creation. So we have once again the search for a 'for ever' awaited in the hope of its revelation.

Catherine said:

> Perhaps I am dreaming . . . like everyone . . . at any rate, that is how it feels when I wake up. But what am I left with? In the end, hardly anything, just a vague impression . . . little bits of blurred pictures. . . . Sparks that flare up and then disappear. Sounds that dissolve into silence. Hollowed-out spaces. All there is when I wake up is a pain in the diaphragm.

I told Catherine that, at this moment, *I* was the person she was telling all this to. Catherine thought for a moment and then said: 'Is telling you about it a way of trying to keep hold of something that has lost all possibility of becoming?'

The analysand was here unwittingly – or, at least, so I saw it – asking one of the key questions of analytic work. 'Telling about it' meant 'talking to oneself' and hence using her own capacity to channel the flood of excitations into representational forms, which could become the enclosure within which those excitations could be grasped. It also meant 'talking to me', and thereby acknowledging my presence, the presence of a body and mind outside her own, as a now necessary reference. She was therefore cathecting representations of an object of needs, wishes and frustrations; when and how these become established as a psychic network has long been a central problem of analytic practice. I am thinking here of Freud's hesitation between, on the one hand, what is rediscovered (memories, traumas, the truth of the past) – i.e., the plot of a substantially prerecorded text which must be remembered – and, on the other, fantasy, everything that is created in the bipersonal relationship of the treatment, the transformations achieved in the transference, which is not a copy but a new production.

This hesitation persisted throughout Freud's career, from the early case histories, through 'The Wolf Man' and *Inhibitions, Symptoms and Anxiety* to 'Analysis terminable and interminable', and remained a matter of controversy among his successors. The question has plainly not been resolved to this day.

All analysts today agree that the formulation of our interpretations demonstrates our acquiescence in Freud's conception of a sexuality that eludes conscious knowledge, and of an unconscious psychic life whose constraints affect the analyst's productions just as much as they do the analysand's; however, interpretations differ considerably according to whether the analyst's aim is to reveal the truth of a past that must be rediscovered, including memories of events in psychic or external reality, or primarily to disclose fantasy and, in particular, to analyse desire and its place in mental life. Whereas some insist on the need to redeem the mortgage on the present constituted by infantile experience and traumatic events, by inducing the ego to appropriate secondary repressed matter (*The Ego and the Id*, 1923), for others the work of analysis is determined by the construct, by what was 'never there' before the establishment of the analytic relationship.[3]

However, today's clinical practice evidently compels us to take a different view. Interpretation is dictated by a concern to open the patient's mind to the infinite range of meanings and to allow association to resume – a concern that gives rise to different interpretative aims and formulations – and becomes primarily a way of making the patient aware that the networks of meanings are unlimited and that their negotiation is not confined to the period of an analysis. In this context, beyond the remembering and the constructions which underlie the therapeutic approach, the problem is to decide whether analytic work is feasible or whether structural modalities in the patient might make it difficult or even impossible. This might be the case with organizations in which insufficiencies of representation are paralleled by the weight of perceptual data or the crushing burden of images; in which fixations to traumas and to masochistic morbidity correspond to deficiencies in the work of psychic transformation; in which the prevalence of compulsive repetition processes thwarts attempts at symbolization; and in which behaviour leading to exhaustion and the dominion of the void betokens decathexis and retreat from representational life.

Is this necessarily a matter of the unrepresented? Of representations which never came into being because they were never cathected by the preconscious–conscious system? Or of representations swamped, shattered and evacuated by the hurricane-like gusts of the drives sweeping away every manifestation of psychic life?

The psychoanalyst need not answer these questions. On the other hand, the problem of what is representable for a patient concerns us greatly. So, too, do the quantity of energy available for cathexis, a quantity which varies with the progression of the analytic relationship; the network of traces in which the function of desire may be discerned; and the pulsations of an inner life at grips with its own movements towards and away from the object. The crucial question in an analysis – what is the patient's psychic situation? – arises on this level. After all, the significance of 'traumatic' experiences can ultimately be evaluated only by their aftereffects and in the light of two factors:

1 the subject's appetite for excitations, or, at any rate, his propensity to allow himself to be exposed to excesses of traumatizing excitations;
2 the violence of the instinctual thrusts, coupled with possible violence of external origin.[4]

The transformation of these crude thrusts into drive charges directed towards the object and on to the subject constitutes what we call psychic work. However, by calling it work, we are also asserting that it is a process that accompanies the constitution of mental life, which it at the same time establishes. And we are further asserting that the drive thrusts are not self-evidently caught up in the toils of this work. This is not only because of the destructive tendencies that may undermine the attempts of the psychic apparatus at binding, but also because the id's claims may be too great, imposing a constant disturbance on a mind seeking to structure itself. As soon as drive activity grows too strong, or is actually unleashed, it becomes a violent force whose increasing power deranges the ego.

Again, even in relatively innocuous circumstances, drive thrusts may be experienced as dangerous owing to the immaturity of the ego's defensive organization. For example, I consider that the representation of the stranger is the end-point of a process that does not only involve the condensation of 'non-mother' representational elements.[5] A traumatizing perception of the stranger should in my view be connected not only with absences of the maternal object but also with the excess excitation sometimes generated by the mother's presence when she intrudes into the autoerotic and hallucinatory activities organized to replace her. When the drive thrust towards the object meets with the desires of that object, excitation may mount to an unbearable pitch.

A twofold threat and danger thus arise in such situations, which are overburdened with both presence and absence, and in which an external reality combines with unmastered drive manifestations.

The child's psychic apparatus will confront this threat in two ways: firstly, by an attempt at evacuation, which reverses the 'familiar' aspect of the mother and condenses it with what does not come from her, thereby organizing the countercathexis of the perception of the anxiety-inducing stranger in a specific manner; and, secondly, by increasingly stable and constant inner countercathexis of the functional activities that structure the ego.

This development is frustrated by the appetite for excitations. Matters are thereby complicated because, although the psychic apparatus faces the danger that its capacity to bind excitations might be overwhelmed by representational and affective contents, it also has an appetite for excitation,[6] which may even exceed the limits set by the need to impart form.

The potential for non-binding to representational forms is inherent in man, because the earliest stages of existence, in the womb and immediately after birth, cannot possibly be embraced by the representational network. This means that we emerge from a representational chasm, which both fascinates and attracts us.[7] On the metapsychological level, as stated, the attraction to this chasm may be of the order of a relationship between agencies, in which the differentiated ego is attracted by primary repressed contents which it will always experience as a hole in its texture. Bion called this 'O'.

At the clinical level, the pursuit of torrential excitations or the tendency to seek exposure to powerful excitations, even if they damage the stuff of the psyche, is directly bound up with masochism and drive defusion. Indeed, we may here observe the pain of re-encountering excitations connected with an experience of discharge that affords unconscious pleasure. However, drive activity may also be found to be relatively unmoderated by the interference of the fusion of the two drives. On another level, omnipotence joins in as well, suggesting that barriers can be ignored if the subject is prepared to pay the price.

On resumption of sessions after a summer holiday break, Catherine mentioned her curious wish to relive the horror of the 'de-shaping' of the content of her thoughts, her need to disavow her thinking being. 'I exist . . . I do not exist . . . .' Here was a limitless space that made her afraid, but also attracted her. She remembered a scene in which her father exhibited his genitals. 'Turn away from it . . . dissociate from it . . . dilute it.' My patient spoke of her hopes: of becoming able to emerge from the torpor of the disowned; of leaving the wasteland behind her; of forming part of a web of luminous images. However, her dreams – when she remembered them – showed me ruined houses, crumbling buildings and yawning chasms.

Another female patient said: 'I have never been able to feel closed. Everything that gets into me makes me panic in case I dissolve or am absorbed.'[8]

At the beginning of the seventh year of his analysis, a male patient decided that he could finally reveal his most intimate secret to me. His analysis had been characterized by 'clastic' episodes of violent acting out towards the members of his family and himself. He called these episodes 'my rages': he really did 'manage things' so that his dissatisfaction and fury 'mounted' to 'bursting' point.[9]

He would then become like a raging madman, after which he would be exhausted, drained of his strength, 'a demolished body', as he put it. Now, for the first time, he disclosed to me that a point would come in these fits when he felt that the contents of his head were bursting out – that his thoughts were fleeing, becoming deformed, unable to withstand the crashing storms of his fury. A heavy, death-like silence would then ensue. Later, 'gradually', he said:

> it is like nature waking up at daybreak . . . I feel as if I have survived the cataclysm, and although it leaves me gasping for breath and drained of strength, it also arouses a profound elation in me. I feel like the creator of a universe that is taking shape.

When excitations overwhelm the psyche so that unbinding tendencies can gain the upper hand, the latter combine with exhaustion-seeking behaviour and may even annihilate the capacity for representation; the psychic apparatus is then drained and silenced. Again, even in the absence of these extreme forms, the representation-free affect of free-floating anxiety, as well as uncanny feelings indicative of moments of non-binding due to the irruption of the repressed, shatter the sense of continuity and of identifying coherence. Yet some patients derive from this very shattering not only a sense of existence but also a feeling of self-creation through catastrophe.

How then is it possible to move on from an exposed, open psychic body, with its vital substance leaking away, to an internal fabric woven from the tangle of defensive configurations and rays emanating from drive activity? Alternatively, how is it possible to achieve the transition from an all-embracing, enclosing and immobilizing sphincter–anus–vagina – i.e., from the stagnation of primary anality – to a sphincter engaged in the anal activity of retaining and expelling? How can the suspensive logic of splits (neither yes nor no), or what seemingly lacks any traces of desire or pleasure, be transformed into the working of a psychic apparatus that wishes to acknowledge and affirm its movements in its relationship with its object world?

Tracing a path

The literature on the therapy of borderline states is so abundant that any attempt to summarize it would be misleading. Narcissistic resistances, difficulties with internalization, splitting processes, mechanisms of projective identification and of idealization (of both object and self), and, in particular, the pursuit of castration together make up a picture that compels us to graft the work of a typical analysis on to a large number of modifying parameters.

Close examination shows that all technical modifications ensue from the need to frustrate the silent – or noisy – workings of destructiveness, with the aim of allowing form and thinkability to be imparted to the tensions which arise out of the compulsion to repeat, and which tend to negate ideational representatives. Framing, supporting, containing, lending one's thought apparatus and representations, reintroducing the foreclosed, eroticizing the traumatic, giving meaning to the asymbolic, naming the desire: all these approaches have the aim of mobilizing the patient's capacity for internal and external binding and for mastering excitations, thereby inhibiting the action of defused destructiveness and libido.

In every case the analyst–analysand dyad embarks upon a prolonged and arduous task, which may sometimes prove fruitless, especially if the narcissism of the analyst unconsciously complements the patient's fantasies. These include the fantasy of immortality that lurks beneath the persistence of the process of hope, which combats castration and death by disavowing the passage of time. This fantasy opposes the authentic pursuit of the object and militates against the unfolding in the transference/countertransference of a network of identifications whereby creative work on a bipersonal basis might be initiated.

Hope appears in the form of a bulwark against psychic mobilization through which change might come about. This is so even if the analytic encounter and the ensuing process are based on the patient's conscious hope of being relieved of his suffering, and on the analyst's hope of being able to accompany the patient along the road of transformation. The analytic play suffers in consequence.[10]

According to D. Winnicott, in order to use an object the subject must have developed a *capacity* to use objects. If an object is to be used, it must be something other than a bundle of projections. Usage cannot be described except in terms of acceptance of the object's independent existence. The object is already placed outside the area of the subject's omnipotent control. It has survived destruction, which means that its destruction was attempted and accomplished without a retaliatory response by the object. This makes it possible for the object to be used in a world of shared reality.[11]

Winnicott is normally credited with the introduction of the idea of play in analytic theory. He defines psychoanalysis as 'a highly specialized form of playing in the service of communication with oneself and others'.[12] He states that psychotherapy is done in the overlap of two play areas, that of the patient and that of the therapist.[13]

Of course, this idea was already present in Freud's mind when he likened the neurotic's use of the fantasy world for replacement or transformation of an unpleasant reality to children's play (1924e, p. 187). His phraseology was even closer to Winnicott's in the following passage dating from 1914: 'We render the compulsion [to repeat] harmless, and indeed useful, by [. . .] [admitting] it into the transference as a playground in which it is allowed to expand in almost complete freedom.'[14] A little later in the same text, he says: 'The transference thus creates an intermediate region between illness and real life through which the transition from the one to the other is made.'

Earlier, in 1907, he had himself provided an example of therapeutic play with his paper on Jensen's Zoe, who consents to be a living Gradiva–Zoe in order to free Hanold from his delusions.[15] However, the practice of analysis shows that participation in analytic play is not always achieved, and that there are patients for whom the interplay of reality and imagination is not possible; analysis for them is mainly an encounter with an external therapeutic object.[16] These subjects very often seek outside themselves the representatives of the superego and of the ego ideal. Because of their dependence on external agencies, some authors have linked this pathology with M. Mahler's phase of separation–individuation. The past in these patients never comes together to form a history. There is only the memory of traumas in the sequence of failures with the objects of desire.

How then is the breaking or interruption of cycles of repetition to be conceived? How is analytic play to be initiated? The modifications of the setting and of technique described by the authors who have considered the problem are attempts to answer this question, and there is no need to enumerate all the proposed solutions again here. Instead, I shall try to outline the elements that seem to me to be taken for granted in all the approaches developed in order to facilitate the introduction and creative use of the process of association and interpretation.

Recent psychoanalytic literature has shown an increasing awareness that the development of the capacity to internalize and the quality of introjections are conditional upon the mother's being to a certain degree open to her child. Freud, Bion, Winnicott and other authors, such as E. Bick, M. Fain, D. Braunschweig and D. Anzieu, have described entities such as the protective shield against stimuli, the capacity for repression, the container function, the ability to tolerate sexual excitation, the possibility of being seduced by one's own psychic functioning (one's thought, fantasies and dreams) without losing oneself in the process, the capacity for individuation and so on. All of these presuppose a mother figure who has introduced the child to the alternation of cathexes and decathexes, of continuity and discontinuity, of instances of sameness and otherness.

From the statements of Freud and his successors on primary and secondary identifications, it is clear that internalizations are constitutive of the ego, which assumes its specific form by internalizing individual experiences and by retaining these formative experiences in the memory. We therefore conceive of the ego as substantially moulded by identificatory internalizations relating to representations of the object. Of course, since what is internalized is not the object but its representations – as they arise in us after transformation by our fantasies – these representations are surely also laden with our own reinternalized projections. However, it is certainly on the basis of the primordial relationship with the mother and with what the mother 'is' – i.e., the bearer of libido cathecting her child – that the latter's ego can take itself as an object, including therein its female carer.[17]

From the *Three Essays* on, Freud refers to the mother as the first seductress who awakens the child to the life of desire. I have postulated with reference to another text, the *Outline*,[18] that for Freud, the mother through her maternal care not only awakens the child to life but also watches over this life which depends on her: by way of a basic tendency which he assigns to the ego, Freud (1940a [1938], p. 199) introduces the function of an internalized mother who 'watches over it'. He says that 'the ego is governed by considerations of safety'. This, of course, has to do not with the biological safety of the organism but with the safety that may result from mastery of conflict.

Starting with the *Project* and then, via the metapsychological papers, in the structural approach of the second theory, Freud makes the ego responsible for watchfulness and also assigns it a particular role, that of mediator in psychic life through the functions of attention, repression and judgement, since the drives that serve sexual pleasure are opposed in the ego to those of self-preservation.

Watchfulness is often deemed to belong to the separate part of the ego which sets itself up as an overseer, the superego. However, my conception of this function is more in line with the definition given by Freud in the *Outline* (1940a [1938], p. 206): 'So long as the ego works in full harmony with the super-ego it is not easy to distinguish between their manifestations.' This he writes after having dwelt at length on the tensions and differences between the functions of ego and superego, their tendencies and so on.

However, in what psychic trends may this concordance be manifested? What type of functioning may it correspond to? At what times does this functioning emerge? How is it to be identified? These are important questions, because the drives in my view attain their highest degree of fusion in this situation; the fusion is much more relative when the agencies of the ego and the superego are separated.

This is surely not a matter of what the ego must do according to the law of the internalized parental superego, or of supervision (the 'other' supervising the ego, the precursor of the superego-to-be), but more of watchfulness in relation to what the psychic apparatus 'can' do for itself, so as to avoid invasion by anxiety or by self-destructive impulses and to enable it to follow its own movements and ultimately acknowledge them.

From the point of view of the mother, the 'watching' function normally assumed by her from the beginning of her child's life is essentially connected with the two aspects of her bisexuality: passivity, in her receptivity to the child's needs, and activity, in attitudes of watchfulness involving the mother's thought as well as her body. The child, for its part, may be said to learn to take care of itself by internalizing the care lavished on it by its mother.

I do not think that Winnicott's primary maternal preoccupation or the primary maternal field[19] cover what I am trying to define. This is firstly because the function concerned is not limited in time, and secondly because it assumes meaning and value only by deferred action after it has been appropriated by the subject's ego during the phase of constitution of the superego dimension.

The role of this function is therefore not confined to the constitution of the primary ego. For this reason, while its roots may be considered in relation to the functions of support, the protective shield against stimuli, primary maternal preoccupation, the mother's reverie (Bion), Winnicott's holding and the concept of buoyancy,[20] it is bound by its emergence to the time when the dynamisms of the ego and superego are laid down.

The specificity of the 'watching' function results from the fact that it has to do not only with the history of the subject's development but also with his structure – i.e., his psychic organization – which may be inferred from the absence or presence of an ego/superego activity having a convergent and not merely a conflictual potential.

In 'Analysis terminable and interminable' (1937c, p. 238), Freud discusses the compulsion to seek out repetitively situations which endanger the ego, and notes that the quantitative element of the drives cannot be coped with if it overwhelms the barriers which the ego can set up against them. The development from the ego of helplessness to the more or less unified and coherent ego capable of stable identifications takes place on the basis of the internalization of early object relations. For this reason, weaknesses of the ego – irrespective of the causes of their emergence – cannot but connote deficiencies in the capacity to internalize and establish in the psychic space a mothering function of watchfulness whereby the subject becomes able to recognize and watch over his own somatopsychic movements.

I therefore postulate that the repetitive seeking-out of danger situations and the tendency for the subject to expose himself to trauma and disorganizing excitations betray a failure on the part of the ego to assume its own maternal 'watching' dimension. It is no coincidence that Freud connected the mother constellation with life as much as with death. From this point of view, the figure of the deadly mother of unbridled pleasures or of destructuring decathexes links up with a psychic configuration open to the repetition compulsion and imbued with the death drive. The other face of the mother figure is what I have called the 'watching mother', and is revealed in attitudes of watchfulness, attention, guarding and defensive prevention which protect the subject in situations he cannot cope with and integrate.

The ego's receptivity to these attitudes is analogous to its capacity to assume and internalize the function of the watching mother by turning back the drive on itself. The subject thus becomes able to watch over himself, in the sense of acquiring the capacity to recognize and follow his own psychic movements, the cathexes exchanged between the psychic agencies and between the ego and its objects.

'Watching' is on the side of life: watching over someone means paying attention to what happens to him so as to be able to intervene if necessary. But watching is also on the side of death: watching over a dead person means to stay with him, not to abandon him, thereby fostering the illusion of putting off the moment when a human system is yielded up for ever to the silence of death.

In my terms, however, the activity of watching has to do principally with psychic life. As both an attitude and a function, 'watching' presupposes the relationship with the unknown, with whatever may arise in the thought and acts of a person, of an analysand or indeed of the analyst. This attitude and function of the analyst are not in my view inconsistent with what we call evenly suspended attention.[21] In fact, I think that both aspects must be present.

We can now ask whether this image of the watching mother results from the repression, or from the reversal into its opposite, of the figure of the perverse seductive mother, like the Jocasta of Sophocles, or the mother who leaves Oedipus, her child, to suffer, like the Epicaste of the Odyssey, out of a secret hate – or perhaps from an inversion of the hybrid femininity of the Sphinx. Or does this image result from the disavowal in ourselves of the monstrous mother described by C. Stein?[22]

I believe the question is unanswerable. The mother, like the analyst, inevitably partakes of both aspects, not only because of the child's (or the analysand's) projections but also, and in particular, by virtue of the psychic constitutions involved. If we say that they partake of both aspects, we are acknowledging the nature of our psychic movements, in which the repressed constantly returns (and that is the favourable case). We are then acknowledging the unceasing alternation within us of the mother of hate and the mother of love. Freud enables us to take this step, which he was unable to take himself because of his own difficulties with the mother transference and with the owning of his femininity.[23]

Conversely, Freud never shrank from naming and reconstructing contradictory and complementary psychic trends: confrontational violence and tokens of love; cruel, sadistic images and reparative guilt; acknowledgement of the harm a person may do to others and himself, and defences against depression.

Man's relationship with his world is full of confrontations between violence and tenderness, fear and seduction, pleasure and suffering, the lust for excitation and the limits imposed on it by representability and the interference of reality as a third element. The buffetings of this journey may disrupt and sometimes even overwhelm psychic life, as our analyses often show. Consequently, if the analysand's ego can assume a watching function over his body, his psychic space, and the movements which take shape and are performed within it, this is indicative of a remobilization in the patient of a mother aspect in the relationship, regardless of the sexes of the analysand and the analyst. This proves that the analysand is in the process of taking responsibility for himself, by accepting separation from his external carers. Of course, this presupposes that the primitive anxieties (both paranoid–schizoid and depressive) have been adequately worked through and that the sense of continuity, identity and psychic coherence is sufficiently established.

For the duration of an analysis, the work is regulated by the setting. The polarities of external space versus psychic space, of a fixed location and fixed bodies versus the movements of thought (internal movements), characterize the institution of analysis, whose space is given a centre by the analyst, providing the permanence of a presence at regular intervals, contrasting with periods of absence.

For some analysands, however – in particular, those with narcissistic pathology – the setting serves primarily as an οἶκος, an enclosed area,[24] in which they build or rebuild their psychic space. The reconstitution of this space, as well as the mobilization of the forces that dwell within it, is not without its perils and is inevitably accompanied by fierce resistances. Acting out, accidents, and negative therapeutic reactions are the painful hazards encountered during the analytic journey, where such a journey proves possible at all.

Interpretative activity is here usually based on the analyst's evenly suspended attention, backed by a watching attitude: watching over the project of analysis in general, and in particular over the analysand's somatopsychic movements; over what goes unsaid; over lacunae, which are not to be filled but to be historicized; over negative inscriptions, which must be transformed; over what cannot be represented or given form, but must be owned; over the excessive and the contradictory; and – last but by no means least – over the emergence of the countertransference out of its burden of unconscious desires, regarded by Ferenczi as unresolved residues of the analyst's own analysis.

This blend of watching and evenly suspended attention, moments of oscillation in the time of our countertransference, in my opinion constitutes the setting for the movements of the analyst's thought. This setting links up and combines with that of space, time and the rules of analysis, and it accompanies and complements the dream model of the work of the session. In Bion's terms, alpha and K elements are deemed to be undamaged in the analyst and always available to him.

Analytic work is done on the basis of withdrawal of the presence and suspension of the conscious thought of the analyst; however, he must be capable of oscillating between the aspect of watching and that of evenly suspended attention if he is to remain open to the drive charges or the 'meaninglessness' present in the analysand while at the same time managing his own countertransference without immediate discharge and while assigning meaning by interpretation. Either of these aspects can be made more readily audible by muting the other. The withdrawal which absents the analyst and the voids made possible by analytic listening are accompanied by the concern inherent in the watching presence, and the one frames the other as they cancel each other out instance by instance at different moments in the analysis. The analyst's 'I am not here', his withdrawal in the face of seduction, is complemented by his watchful, caretaking presence in a setting open to transgressions and spurious passion.

On the subject of the infantile, A. Green wrote that the mother must steer a course between the 'too much' and the 'not enough'. The same applies to the analyst: what matters is the extent to which the analysand articulates absence – for instance, silence or separations – with presence, and what he is able to do with it in the process of integrating the call to meaning inherent in interpretations, which, by introducing exploration of the byways of absence, arouse feelings of anxiety, guilt and narcissistic loss.

A female analysand mentioned her wish to go to sleep during a session, and noted that she was finally able to trust me. 'Perhaps it is because I can trust myself', she said. 'If I fall asleep, that means that you will stay awake and will wake me up when the time comes' (this is to be understood also in the metaphorical sense of a call to meaning at the appropriate time). A male patient said: 'Now I have to protect my joy.'

Generally valid as these considerations are, I believe they are even more relevant to analysands with narcissistic pathology, in whom splits in thought, and between thought and what happens in the soma or is acted out, are particularly tenacious and dangerous to psychic life. For this very reason they call for the 'watching' presence of the analyst,[25] because these patients, who react strongly to discontinuities in the analytic relationship, often fiercely disavow the existence of their separation anxiety; at the same time they experience discontinuities as a loss of attention and interest on the part of the psychoanalyst, so that their very existence is threatened. For them, discontinuities are evidence of the analyst's unreliability.

Freud said that little was known about the process of overcoming repetition. However, we may be able to understand the problem better by considering the types of negative therapeutic reaction which cannot be explained solely in terms of moral masochism, but are due to the very low level of drive fusion, which is responsible for the primary violence of self-destructuring and self-destructive impulses and for the demoniacal force of repetition. Here the main aim of repetition is not mastery but exhaustion of the energy of cathexes.

Hence, whereas the complete overcoming of repetition seems to be an illusory goal, breaches in the cycle and some relaxation of resistances may flow from the relationship with an external object which encourages countercathexis of the void, of internal destruction and of the experience of the object as destructive, and which introduces notions of differentiation by the alternations of its attitude between 'watching' and evenly suspended attention. The mobilization of a capacity for fantasized eroticization of the bodies of the subject and of the other so as to facilitate the emergence of thing-representations with the capacity to become word-representations is, of course, secondary to this relationship to the object.

Searles said that 'therapeutic symbiosis' was the necessary form of relationship with the object in difficult cases. Winnicott mentioned a kind of holding that could extend into external reality (cf. M. Little's case). On the basis of my personal experience – no doubt because my patients' pathology was not so severe – I would say that it is not always necessary to go to such lengths.

Through the blending of two contrasting attitudes in the analyst, 'watching' and evenly suspended attention, linked with words standing for the excluded representations and affects, it becomes possible to introduce elements of difference, whereby the tightly woven fabric of psychic non-differentiations in the relationship with external and internal reality can be loosened, thus initiating a process in which repetition of the identical can be reduced.

The refusion of drives can begin by the use of masochism, while the possible mitigation of the narcissistic transference – whereby the grandiose ideal may be transformed into father and mother imagos – may induce the patient to embark on a process of mourning. If progress is then made towards internalization of the function of the analyst as both the 'watching' mother and the working and seeking father mentioned by M. Fain, it may be hoped that the patient will ultimately arrive at conceptions of himself and his objects in which he recognizes the productions of his thought as his own; these productions will be tolerable, though always deficient, compared with his desire for knowledge and total presence. Omnipotent fantasies may well recede.

It will then become possible for constructions to replace the lost ideal, in which the process of hoping is involved, and the patient may be able to establish a form of contact with the outside/inside that will enable him to create with the analyst what I have called his myth/historical truth (Potamianou, 1984); for the *moira* of every analysis is, after all, irrevocably bound up with abandonment of the enclosed analytic space and with the extent of the analysand's openness to traffic with the obscure, the unrepresentable, the different, and the alien within him.

Notes

Introduction

1 Clement of Alexandria, *Stromateis*, II, 17, 4. If he does not hope, he will not find the unhoped for, which does not lend itself to investigation and cannot be traversed.

2 Ibid, p. 8.

3 These cases admittedly often give the impression of a dynamic constellation, thus, for many authors justifying the use of the term 'borderline states' rather than 'borderline organization'. However, I do not think it necessary to deem permanence to be an attribute of an organization, any more than to regard a 'state' as something provisional (see D. Widlöcher's foreword to the French edition of O. Kernberg's study, published by Privat as *Les troubles limites de la personnalité*, 1979, p. 9). I consider that either term may be used, provided that (a) the concept of organization is given its full dynamic valence and (b) it is agreed that what is to be denoted is a predominant configuration in the subject's mental life. There may then, of course, be very substantial fluctuations over time, with many possible combinations of symptoms.

4 D. Winnicott (1968), 'The use of an object and relating through identification', in *Playing and Reality*, London, Penguin Books, 1971.

5 It should be added here that narcissistic disorders in borderline patients become manifest over a range extending from grandiose appreciation of the self to lack of self-esteem; profound self-concern and egocentric interests coexist with an absence of empathy in relations with others – although this does not mean that the other's point of view goes unnoticed during interaction. Relations with external objects are governed by intense needs for gratification, which makes for interpersonal relations in which obedience and submission far outweigh the internalization and critical evaluation of moral values.

Within the large category of borderline states, O. Kernberg (1975, p. 17) identifies the group of so-called narcissistic personalities as patients who are not severely regressed but whose emotional life is shallow. Most of these cases have an underlying borderline organization. Kernberg notes that patients classified as having a narcissistic structure are amenable to analytic treatment, which, however, he considers inappropriate for other borderline organizations in which psychotic aspects are more marked (O. Kernberg, 'Transference regression and psychoanalytic technique with infantile personalities', *International Journal of Psycho-Analysis*, 1991, 72: 189–207).

6 To clarify my views on certain points, I shall sometimes use material from earlier publications.

Chapter 1 Hope as a binding cathexis

1 Quotations from Hesiod are taken from the OUP *World's Classics*, 1988 edition, translated by M.L. West, Oxford and New York, Oxford University Press.

2 West's translation says 'made', but the Greek word ἐξαγαγε literally means 'to cause to emerge'.

3 See J. Harrison (1962 and 1980), *Prolegomena to the Study of Greek Religion*, London, Merlin Press, p. 284, and the comments in *Greek Mythology*, Athens, Ekdotiki, vol. 2, pp. 57–58. J. Harrison notes that Hesiod diminished the importance of the great Earth Goddess and placed more emphasis on the Olympian gods, ruled by a father figure.

4 Hesiod, *Works and Days*, line 94.

5 See A. Potamianou (1979), 'Réflexions psychanalytiques sur la Prométhia d'Eschyle', in *Psychanalyse et Culture grecque*, Paris, Belles-Lettres, 1980.

6 *Works and Days*, lines 85–89.

7 As J.-P. Vernant notes, 'men will henceforth no longer be born direct from the earth. With woman, they will know birth by begetting, and consequently also ageing, pain and death'. See J.-P. Vernant (1965), *Mythe et pensée chez les Grecs*, Paris, Maspero, p. 187.

8 Aeschylus, *Prometheus Bound*, line 250. Translated by D. Grene. In 'The Complete Greek Tragedies', edited by D. Grene and R. Lattimore, *Aeschylus II*, Chicago and London, University of Chicago Press, 1956.

9 'Ημαρτον' connotes equally 'fault' and 'mistake'.

10 *Works and Days*, line 48.

11 See A. Potamianou, op. cit.

12 J.-P. Vernant, op. cit., p. 38.

13 C. Stein (1987), *Les Erinyes d'une mère. Essai sur la haine*, Paris, Calligrammes.

14 J. Harrison, op cit., p. 281.

15 When the Avars besieged Constantinople in AD 626, while Emperor Heraclius was away fighting the Persians, the patriarch Sergius, followed by the entire population, celebrated a night-time mass in the church of Vlachernai. The congregation remained standing throughout the mass, which went on all night; then, with the icon of the Virgin as their guide, they attacked the Avars and forced them to raise the siege.

16 A. Toynbee (1959), *Hellenism, The History of a Civilization*, London, Oxford University Press, p. 210.

17 See I. Barande (1977), *Le maternel singulier*, Paris, Aubier-Montaigne, p. 103. Ilse Barande says that diachrony is here transformed into synchrony or is reversed (see pp. 90 and 92).

18 C. Stein (1983), Trois allégories de la puissance maternelle, in 'Figurations du féminin', *Etudes freudiennes*, 21–22, Paris, Evel, p. 55.

19 T. Xydis (1978), *Hymnographie Byzantine*, Athens, Nikodimos. The hymn was first published by Aldos Manoutios in 1502.

20 'Nymph' can mean young woman as well as bride.

21 C. Paparrigopoulos (1932), *Histoire de la nation Grecque*, Athens, Eleftheroudakis, vol. III, p. 195.

22 T. Xydis, op. cit., p. 170.

23 Extracts from the *Akathist*. Translated by N. Michael Vaporis and Evie Zachariades-Holmberg, Holy Cross Orthodox Press, Brookline, Mass., 1992.

24 Χαῖρε means 'hail' or 'rejoice'.

25 See D. Stein (1985), *Lectures psychanalytiques de la Bible*, Paris, Les Editions du Cerf, especially Chapter 2, which refers to certain representations of Mary in Biblical texts.

26 Invoking omnipotence does not mean that a homology is assumed between infantile and pathological experience, as Drew Westen says in 'Towards a revised theory of borderline object relations: contributions of empirical research', *International Journal of Psycho-Analysis*, 71, 4: 663. Furthermore, the interference of the various aetiological factors cannot be linked to a specific phase of development.

27 D.W. Winnicott (1954), 'Metapsychological and clinical aspects of regression', in *Through Paediatrics to Psychoanalysis*, London, Tavistock Publications, 1958, p. 281.

Chapter 2 Clinical and metapsychological background

1 The transformation takes place when a threshold is exceeded (Freud, 1950c [1895], p. 108). This energy will from then on have a psychic fate. Permutation of its aims and objects introduces the possibility of a primary symbolization under the aegis of the pleasure principle.

2 Note that, after the 1920 text, Freud often uses the term 'destruction' (of self and of others), which greatly inspired the thought of Melanie Klein and Wilfred Bion.

3 Cf. J. Begoin (1989) 'La violence du désespoir', *Revue française de Psychanalyse*, 53(2): 620.

4 G. Rosolato (1987), *Le sacrifice. Repères psychanalytiques*, Paris, PUF, pp. 20 and 21.

5 See, for example, the various positions adopted by the authors of the contributions in vol. 53 (1989) of the *Revue française de Psychanalyse*.

6 A. Potamianou (1987), 'De vortex et de volcans', *Topique*, 39: 57.

7 S. Freud (1911b), 'Formulations on the two principles of mental functioning', *Standard Edition*, 12, p. 221.

8 Cf. the approach of P. and M. Luquet (1987) in their paper 'La formation du système préconscient et les matériaux de la pensée', *Revue française de Psychanalyse* 2: 751–774.

9 A. Potamianou (1986), 'Des origines du refoulement et de l'agencement des défenses', in *Revue française de Psychanalyse*, 1: 521.

10 See the text quoted above on the origins of repression.

11 [*Translator's note*: The French word *démarcant* used by the author can also mean 'removing the marks from'. This is relevant to point b at the end of this sentence.] The paper by Guy Rosolato on the fate of the signifier was published in the same year (*Nouvelle Revue Psychanalyse*, 1984, 30); he also used the term '*démarcation*', although in a different sense. I felt that there are some words which it is simply not possible to avoid, probably because they convey certain ideas best. G. Rosolato uses the word in a sense that links it to the field of mental images having to do with a referent or with a linguistic signifier, once language has been acquired. My 'demarcating sensations' indicate the sources of thought in the body and lie at the root of ego differentiation.

12 A. Green (1990), 'De l'objet non unifiable à la fonction objectalisante', *Bulletin de la Fédération européenne Psychanalyse*, Vienna symposium.

13 P. Marty (1976, 1980), *Les mouvements individuels de vie et de mort*, Paris, Payot.

14 As clinical experience shows in crude instances of acting out or in certain types of somatizations, the conflict is between the maintenance of a degree of excitability in the form of desire and the reduction of its tension with the aim of reducing excitations to zero.

15 The occupation of a territory (*Besetzung*), which Freud imagined in connection with cathexes, precludes neither the changeability afforded by displacements nor the transformation and reorganization resulting from circulation through the various psychic levels. This is borne out by the fact that countercathexes ultimately use the energy released by derivatives maintained in the unconscious through the cathexis of defensive operations and substitutive formations. The situation becomes rigidly fixed in pathological forms of mourning or where the affect is expressed mono-lithically (e.g., in certain states of love). Differences in cathexes are usually manifested in changes in associations, inhibition of mental activity, etc., because the excess excitation may perform either a stimulating or an inhibiting function in the psychic apparatus.

16 In the second topography, countercathexes are connected not with repression but mainly with ego resistances (Freud, 1926d [1925], Addendum I).

17 G. Painchaud and N. Montgrain (1986), 'Limites et états limites', in *Narcissisme et états limites*, pp. 28–35.

18 A. Potamianou (1989), 'Réflexions et hypothèses sur la problématique des états limites', Colloque de la *Société Psychanalytique de Paris*, January and (1990) *La Psychanalyse: Questions pour demain*, Monographies de la *Revue Française de Psychanalyse*, Paris, PUF.

19 These are situations on the very frontiers of the psychic realm, involving direct discharges in the soma and acts unsupported by fantasization. This does not mean that the dynamic of other repetitions guided by pleasure-seeking is absent in these cases.

20 My distinction between the search for constancy and that for Nirvana is relevant here (Chapter 2, third section, p. 51).

21 A. Potamianou (1988), 'Un aspect du maternel: la fonction de veilleuse', second Psychoanalytic Symposium, Delphi, Greece.

22 A. Green was also referring to this in his discussion of the archaic; see *Nouvelle Revue de Psychanalyse*, 1982, 26: 211.

23 [*Translator's note*: Published translation modified.]

24 Borderlines are quick to perceive and experience objects as having baneful intentions.

25 Anything that becomes separate and differentiates itself necessarily turns bad, because it is outside the self and out of control, and also because it absorbs projections of fantasy.

26 See Chapter 2, first section, p. 18.

27 See P. Luquet's (1962) important contribution, 'Les identifications précoces dans la structuration et la restructuration du Moi', *Revue française de Psychanalyse*, 26 Numéro spécial; and A. de Mijolla (1981), *Les visiteurs du Moi. Fantasmes d'identification*, Paris, Les Belles-Lettres.

28 See F. Pasche (1965), 'Notes sur l'investissement', in *A partir de Freud*, Paris, Payot, 1969, pp. 243–248.

29 A. Potamianou (1985), 'A propos du deuxième courant pulsionnel', in *Bulletin de la Fédération européenne de Psychanalyse*, 25: 89–93. These are patients whose ego organization remains intact – i.e., they can function in accordance with the reality principle – until profound regressive tendencies appear during significant phases of the analysis.

30 A. Potamianou (1983), 'Sur quelques modalités de la régression', *Topique*, 31: 91–104.

31 Is this because the object already proved deficient in the primary relationship? Did it perhaps deeply wound the subject's nascent narcissism? A. Green (1986, p. 22), referring to Winnicott, mentions absence which leads to despair because the object can exist only through the disappointment or unpleasure which it generates. However, that object cannot be abandoned, owing to the constant demand for the love of which it has deprived the subject, the hate it arouses, and the associated guilt.

32 Callimachus, Hymn III: To Artemis, in *Callimachus, Hymns, Epigrams, Select Fragments*, translated by S. Lombardo and D. Rayor, Johns Hopkins University Press, Baltimore and London, 1988, pp. 11 and 12.

33 I. Prigogine and I. Stengers (1986) *La Nouvelle Alliance*, Paris, Gallimard, 1979. [Translator's note: This work was completely rewritten for its English edition, *Order out of Chaos. Man's New Dialogue with Nature*, published by Bantam Books Inc., USA, 1984. The passages quoted here have been translated by the present translator.]

34 A. Potamianou (1987), 'De vortex et de volcans', in *Topique*, 39: 49–61.

35 This is what Freud (1926d [1925], Addendum C, p. 171) meant by the following sentence: 'The transition from physical pain to mental pain corresponds to a change from narcissistic cathexis to object-cathexis.'

36 S. Freud (1950c [1895]), Draft G. 'Melancholia', *Standard Edition*, 1, pp. 205–206.

37 See A. Potamianou (1987), op. cit., p. 56.

38 Callimachus, op. cit., lines 26 and 42–44.

39 Freud always remained faithful to the position that as long as life persists, the drives are observable only in alloyed form, except at moments when they undergo defusion. Referring to the two drives, Freud (1926d [1925], p. 125) wrote: 'We are concerned with . . . mixtures in various proportions.' Note that Freud himself hardly ever uses the word *Verschmelzung* (fusion) to denote the manner of combination of the drives, but mentions *Mischung* (mixture) or

Legierung (alloy). The standard English technical terms 'fusion' and 'defusion', although used in this translation, are in my view misleading; I consider that 'mixing' and 'unmixing' would be more accurate renderings of Freud's *Mischung* and *Entmischung* in relation to drives.

40 B. Rosenberg (1989), 'Pulsion de la mort et intrication pulsionnelle', *Revue française de Psychanalyse*, 53(2): 557–575.

41 The case of Catherine is an example. The term 'non-fusion of drives' should be understood as corresponding clinically to manifestations in which destructiveness and (both object-related and narcissistic) libidinal cathexes are unmitigated by mixtures that attenuate their manifestations.

42 B. Rosenberg (1989), op. cit., p. 564.

43 A. Potamianou (1990), p. 176.

44 S. Freud (1923a [1922]), Libido theory, in 'Two encyclopaedia articles', *Standard Edition*, 18, p. 258.

45 Patients are aware of their difficulties in maintaining affective cathexes. This explains their intense abandonment and separation anxieties – which result from projective activity – and their high sensitivity to losses.

46 A. Potamianou (1988), 'Figurations du Nirvâna et réaction thérapeutique négative', *Revue française de Psychanalyse*, 4: 917–933. This patient was a man aged 37, who had always been very susceptible to somatic disorders. He had had episodes of allergic dermatitis, intestinal troubles and stomach spasms from an early age. He was subject to attacks of fever which could not readily be diagnosed and which the doctors vaguely attributed to a virus. However, Mr R was not bothered by his susceptibility to somatic disorders. What he wanted to understand and change were his homosexual tendencies and his fears, which were at times tantamount to phobias. The patient had career inhibitions and found it hard to form lasting relationships.

He maintained impressive splits between his psychic apparatus and anything somatic, as well as in regard to his parental imagos and the representation of his self (weak, dependent and respectful, while at the same time having the power to influence other people's lives by his thought and eloquence). The masochistic dimension was very pronounced. His dreams and fantasy productions betrayed a low level of preconscious censorship, so that the unconscious could reveal itself as overstimulating. There was an obvious craving for painful excitations.

47 See Jean Laplanche's approach to this problem, in *Vie et mort en psychanalyse*, Paris, Flammarion, 1970, p. 198.

48 M. de M'Uzan (1972), 'Un cas de masochisme pervers', in *La sexualité perverse*, Paris, Payot, p. 41.

49 K. Abraham (1919), 'A particular form of neurotic resistance against the psycho-analytic method', in *Selected Papers on Psycho-Analysis*, translated by D. Bryan and A. Strachey, London, Hogarth Press, 1949, pp. 303–311.

50 A. Potamianou (1988), op. cit.

51 A. Green (1990), *Narcissisme et masochisme*, Berne lecture.

52 See Chapter 2, third section, p. 26.

53 S. Freud (1914g), 'Remembering, repeating and working-through', *Standard Edition*, 12, p. 151.

54 For the role of this first-couple relationship in the analytic situation, see B. Grunberger (1979).

55 See B. Rosenberg (1982) on deadly masochism and masochism as the guardian of life.

Chapter 3 Hope

1 Letter of 5 January 1913, quoted by E. Jones, *Sigmund Freud, Life and Work*, vol. II, 1955, p. 168.

2 Letter of 17 January 1938, in: *Letters of Sigmund Freud 1873–1939*, edited by Ernst L. Freud, translated by T. and J. Stern, London, Hogarth Press, 1961, p. 436.

3 Euripides, *Helen*, translated by R. Lattimore, in *Euripides II, The Complete Greek Tragedies*, edited by D. Grene and R. Lattimore, University of Chicago Press.

4 G. Bompiani (1986), 'L'attente de la mort et du miracle', *Nouvelle Revue de Psychanalyse*, 34: 140.

5 H. Boris (1976), 'On hope: its nature and psychotherapy', in *International Review of Psycho-Analysis*, 3: 139–150.

6 R. Spitz (1945), 'Hospitalism', in *Psychoanalytic Study of the Child*, vol. 1, New York, International Universities Press.

7 M. Fain and P. Marty (1964), 'A propos du narcissisme et de sa genèse', *Revue française de Psychanalyse*, 1965, 29: 561–572.

8 J. Chasseguet-Smirgel (1985), pp. 206–209. F. Pasche (1973) drew attention to the need to specify one's meaning when referring to this project (*Revue française de Psychanalyse*, 5–6: 1020).

9 J. Begoin (1989), 'La violence du désespoir ou le contre-sens d'une pulsion de mort en psychanalyse', *Revue française de Psychanalyse*, 2: 619–640.

10 See J. Chasseguet-Smirgel (1985), p. 30.

11 Ibid, p. 31.

12 A. Haynal (1976), 'Le sens du désespoir', *Revue française Psychanalyse*, 1977, 1–2: 103 and 104.

13 L. Altman (1957), 'The waiting syndrome', *Psychoanalytic Quarterly*, 26(4): 508–518.

14 S. Freud (1927c), *The Future of an Illusion, Standard Edition* 21, p. 49 (rearranged).

15 The extracts from Homer's *Odyssey* are taken from the edition translated by R. Lattimore, published in New York by Harper & Row.

16 N. Kazantzakis (1938), *Odysseas*, Athens, Stochastis; here translated from the author's French version.

17 J.-P. Vernant (1989), *L'individu, la mort, l'amour*, Paris, Gallimard, p. 146.

18 This certainly does not mean that the process of hope cannot be cathected defensively.

19 E. Bergler (1939), 'On the psychoanalysis of the ability to wait and of impatience', *Psychoanalytic Review*, 26: 11–32.

20 *Holy Bible*, authorized King James version, Isaiah, Chapters XL, XLI and XLII.

21 N. Kazantzakis (1928), *Christos*, Athens, Stochastis, p. 101.

22 *The Divine Liturgy of Saint John Chrysostom*, Holy Cross Orthodox Press, Brookline, Massachusetts.

23 The Swiss painter Cuno Amiet's picture *Espoir* [*Hope*] (1902) is a good

illustration of the alloying of the drives. It shows a woman standing with her hands spread wide, like the Indian chief in *The Appeal to the Great Spirits* by the American sculptor Cyrus Dallin (1862–1944). A newborn baby can be seen below the woman, and a dead man and woman on either side of her.

24 'Oedipus the King', translated by D. Grene, in *Sophocles I, The Complete Greek Tragedies*, edited by D. Grene and R. Lattimore, University of Chicago Press, 1954.

25 *The Divine Liturgy of Saint John Chrysostom*, Holy Cross Orthodox Press, Brookline, Massachusetts.

26 S. Freud (1890a [formerly 1905b]), 'Psychical treatment', *Standard Edition*, 7, p. 289.

27 K. Menninger (1959), 'Hope', *American Journal of Psychiatry*, 111: 481–491; P. Pruyser (1963), 'Phenomenology and dynamics of hoping', *Journal for the Scientific Study of Religion*, 3: 86–96; J. Frank (1968), 'The role of hope in psychotherapy', *International Journal of Psychiatry*, 120: 383–395; A. Weisman (1970), 'Misgivings and misconceptions in the psychiatric care of terminal patients', *Psychiatry*, 33: 67–81.

28 This was a study of groups of parents and children who attended a guidance clinic in Philadelphia. N. Van Dyke (1962), 'Discomfort and hope: their relationship and outcome', *Smith College Studies*, 32: 205–219.

29 'The Suppliant Maidens' (lines 385–386), translated by S.G. Benardete, in *Aeschylus II, The Complete Greek Tragedies*, edited by D. Grene and R. Lattimore, University of Chicago Press, 1956.

Chapter 4 Hopeful waiting in borderline states

1 See Chapter 2, third section, p. 41.

2 S. Freud (1937c), 'Analysis terminable and interminable', *Standard Edition*, 23, pp. 242–243.

3 P. Pruyser, op. cit., p. 88. (See Chapter 3, note 27.)

4 E. Favarel-Garrigues (1986), 'Passager clandestin', *Nouvelle Revue de Psychanalyse*, 34: 149.

5 M. Khan (1973), 'The role of illusion in the analytic space and process', in *The Annual of Psychoanalysis*, vol. I, New York, New York Times Book Co., pp. 231–246.

6 A. Green (1986), *L'aventure négative*, *Nouvelle Revue de Psychanalyse*, 34: 198.

7 E. Bergler, op. cit. (See Chapter 3, note 19.) A. Goldberg (1971), 'On waiting', *International Journal of Psycho-Analysis*, 52: 413–421.

8 Quoted by Goldberg, op. cit.

9 E. Bergler, op. cit., p. 11.

10 C. David (1989), 'La quête de délimitation', *Nouvelle Revue de Psychanalyse*, 40: 173.

11 A. Goldberg, op cit., p. 418.

12 E. Bergler, op. cit., p. 21.

13 B. Favarel-Garrigues (1986), op. cit., p. 143.

14 S. Freud (1919h), 'The "Uncanny"', *Standard Edition*, 17, p. 241.

15 I. Hermann (1976 [1936]), 'Clinging – going-in-search: a contrasting pair of

instincts and their relation to sadism and masochism', *Psychoanalytic Quarterly*, 45: 5–36.

16 M. Masud Khan (1979), *Alienation in Perversions*, London, Hogarth Press.

17 M. de M'Uzan (1972), 'Un cas de masochisme pervers', in *La sexualité perverse*, Paris, Payot, p. 45.

18 O. Kernberg (1975, p. 124) even invokes the deployment of a self-destructive ideology; he considers that self-destruction takes the place of an ego ideal, with severe forms of aggression turned against the self.

19 B. Rosenberg (1982), 'Culpabilité et masochisme moral ou la culpabilité comme négatif du masochisme', in *Masochismes*, Cahiers du Centre de Psychanalyse et de Psychothérapie, 4: 73–110.

20 E. Jones points out that patients labouring under the burden of an unusually powerful unconscious sense of guilt, too painful to be allowed to penetrate into consciousness, may suffer consciously from a sense of inferiority. This complex is described by Freud as the erotic aspect of the sense of guilt. E. Jones (1957), *Sigmund Freud: Life and Work*, vol. 3, London, Hogarth Press, p. 307.

21 S. Kierkegaard (1955 [1849]), *The Sickness unto Death*, New York, Doubleday.

22 Except in the pantheon of the Greek gods.

23 See Chapter 2, third section, p. 41.

24 S. Freud (1908e [1907]), 'Creative writers and day-dreaming', *Standard Edition*, 9, p. 145.

25 S. Freud (1930a [1929]), *Civilization and its Discontents, Standard Edition*, 21, p. 79.

26 See J. Chasseguet-Smirgel (1985), p. 30.

27 See Chapter 2, third section, p. 41.

28 It has to be destroyed if it proves to have boundaries that separate.

29 In terms of the first topography, this would mean a psychic apparatus able to tolerate registration in both systems.

30 C. David (1972), 'La perversion affective', in *La sexualité perverse*, Paris, Payot.

31 C. David, op. cit., p. 215.

32 The dynamic of this process can be traced through A. Green's objectifying function [*fonction objectalisante*] ('*La pulsion de mort*', Paris, PUF, 1984, pp. 55–56). This author postulates the existence of an objectifying function, as distinct from the object relationship, to be considered in its relation to Eros and to the death drive. In this conception, he takes the view that what no longer bears a relation to the primary objects except by meaningful cathexis and by symbolization through metonymy and metaphor is transformed into an object. An objectifying function is revealed in analytic treatment. Green maintains in this context that this objectifying function, which is essentially a striving of the life drives, not only has the role of creating a relationship with the object, whether internal or external, but also proves capable of transforming structures into objects, even when the object is no longer directly involved. This function therefore elevates to the status of an object something that possesses none of the qualities, properties and attributes of the object, provided that just one characteristic – namely, that of meaningful cathexis – is preserved in the psychic work performed.

33 L. Shengold recently discussed anality as a defence against destructiveness in narcissistic regressions. See L. Shengold (1985), 'Defensive anality and anal narcissism', *International Journal of Psycho-Analysis*, 66, 1: 47–73.

Chapter 5 Even God needs a mother

1 Translated by R. Warner, in 'The Complete Greek Tragedies', edited by D. Grene and R. Lattimore, *Euripides I*, Chicago and London, University of Chicago Press, 1955.

2 A. Chekhov, *The Seagull*, Act I and Act III; in: *Plays*, translated by E. Fen, Harmondsworth, Penguin Books, 1951.

3 S. Viderman (1970), '*La construction de l'espace analytique*', Paris, Denoël.

4 P. Aulagnier-Castoriadis (1975) described the trials to which the emerging 'I' may be exposed: negation of the child's knowledge, ability and thought, as well as the imposition of a series of preformative statements which name what is experienced. See also A. Green (1990, p. 30) on the active role of the parental objects in the structuring of the conflict.

5 In accordance with C. Le Guen's conception as described in *Pratique de la méthode psychanalytique*, Paris, PUF, 1982, pp. 94–95.

6 S. Freud, (1905d), *Three Essays on the Theory of Sexuality, Standard Edition*, 7.

7 See also Chapter 2, third section, p. 41.

8 This may be compared with the dream of a neurotic female patient about an open bag which people can look into, mess about in, and look for things inside.

9 This is reminiscent of the logic of dissipative structures in physics, mentioned by I. Prigogine and I. Stengers (op. cit., p. 425, see Chapter 2, note 33). The borderline psyche seems to me to resemble what physicists today call a 'system in a critical state' – i.e., one that does not form stable, harmonious units but assumes a literally unrepresentable condition, in which each event has effects that propagate throughout the system. Fluctuations may consequently be amplified and in certain circumstances, beyond a certain threshold of instability, dissipative activity becomes manifest.

10 Analytic play may be conceptualized on a number of different intersecting planes:

    1 the forms assumed by presence/absence (visual and aural; silence and interpretation); these may be observed in the *fort-da* game described by Freud and in Winnicott's conception of the oscillation between acceptance and rejection;

    2 space in its twofold internal and external aspect;

    3 the twofold movement of the transference: the patient's transference and analyst's countertransference;

    4 the retrograde path from the conscious/preconscious to the domain of the unconscious;

    5 the model of negation–affirmation, no–yes, no and yes.

11 D. Winnicott (1971), 'The use of an object', in *Playing and Reality*, London, Penguin Books, pp. 103–108.

12 Ibid, p. 48.

13 Ibid, p. 63.

14 S. Freud (1914g), 'Remembering, repeating and working-through', *Standard Edition*, 12, p. 154.

15 S. Freud, (1907a [1906]), 'Delusions and dreams in Jensen's *Gradiva*', *Standard Edition*, 9, p. 21.

16 See A. Potamianou (1978), 'Comme on l'utilisera', *Revue française de Psychanalyse*, 1: 111–122. Also (1990): 'Rêves et somatisation', *Topique*, 45: 49–62.

17 See P. Luquet, *'Les identifications précoces'*, op. cit. (See Chapter 3, note 27.)

18 A. Potamianou (1988), 'Un aspect du maternel: la fonction de veilleuse', second Psychoanalytic Symposium, Delphi.

19 F. Begoin-Guignard (1986), 'Le sourire du chat; réflexions sur le féminin', in 'Le féminin maternel', *Bulletin Société Psychanalytique de Paris*, 9: 3–20. See also (1987): 'A l'aube du maternel et du féminin', *Revue française de Psychanalyse*, 6: 1491–1503.

20 This concept is due to J.-M. Quinodoz. See, for example, *The Taming of Solitude*, translated by P. Slotkin, London and New York, Routledge, 1993.

21 Evenly suspended attention is equivalent to the withdrawal of the sustained attention of consciousness.

22 C. Stein (1987), *Les Erinyes d'une mère. Essai sur la haine*, Paris, Calligrammes, p. 40.

23 In relation to the fantasy of self-creation, I. Barande writes: '*He* is not involved in the matter . . . and above all not as the sole begetter, father and mother merged into one. . . . He is the disciple. . . . And certainly not that maternal substance, the principle of everything human.' (I. Barande, 1977, *Le maternel singulier. Freud et Léonard de Vinci*, Paris, Aubier Montaigne, p. 128).

24 Others might see it as a metaphor of the enveloping body of the mother.

25 This is plainly remote from the psychic encroachment by the patient on the analyst which M. de M'Uzan (1976) describes (*Revue française de Psychanalyse*, p. 3). However, the assumption of the alert state may have to do with what the analyst experiences as a deficiency in the patient's capacity for representation.

Selected bibliography

Adler G. (1985) *Borderline Psychopathology and its Treatment*. London: Jason Aronson.
Aulagnier-Castoriadis, P. (1975) *La violence de l'interprétation*. Paris: PUF, Collection 'Le Fil rouge'.
Bergeret, J. (1974) *La dépression et les états limites*. Paris: Payot.
—— and Reid, W. (1986) *Narcissisme et états limites*. Dunod and Presses de l'Université de Montréal.
Bion, W. (1957) 'Differentiation of the psychotic from the non psychotic personalities'. *International Journal of Psycho-Analysis*, 38: 266–275.
—— (1961) *Experiences in Groups* and other papers. London: Tavistock Publications.
—— (1963) *Elements of Psycho-Analysis*. London: Heinemann.
Chasseguet-Smirgel, J. (1985) *The Ego Ideal: A Psychoanalytic Essay on the Malady of the Ideal*. Trans. P. Barrows. London: Free Associations Books.
Freud, S. (1894a) 'The neuro-psychoses of defence'. *The Standard Edition of the Complete Psychological Works of Sigmund Freud*, ed. James Strachey, 24 volumes, London: Hogarth Press, 1953–73, vol. 3.
—— (1895b) 'On the grounds for detaching a particular syndrome from neurasthenia under the description "anxiety neurosis"'. *Standard Edition*, 3.
—— (1914c) 'On narcissism: an introduction'. *Standard Edition*, 14.
—— (1915c) 'Instincts and their vicissitudes'. *Standard Edition*, 14.
—— (1915e) 'The unconscious'. *Standard Edition*, 14.
—— (1916–17f [1915]) 'A metapsychological supplement to the theory of dreams'. *Standard Edition*, 14.
—— (1916–17g [1915]) 'Mourning and melancholia'. *Standard Edition*, 14.
—— (1920g) *Beyond the Pleasure Principle*. *Standard Edition*, 18.
—— (1924e) 'The loss of reality in neurosis and psychosis'. *Standard Edition*, 19.
—— (1925h) 'Negation'. *Standard Edition*, 19.
—— (1926d [1925]) *Inhibitions, Symptoms and Anxiety*. *Standard Edition*, 20.
—— (1927e) 'On fetishism'. *Standard Edition*, 21.
—— (1930a [1929]) *Civilization and its Discontents*. *Standard Edition*, 21.
—— (1933a) *New Introductory Lectures on Psycho-Analysis*. *Standard Edition*, 22.
—— (1937c) *Analysis Terminable and Interminable*. *Standard Edition*, 23.
—— (1939a [1934–38]) *Moses and Monotheism*. *Standard Edition*, 23.
—— (1940a [1938]) *An Outline of Psycho-Analysis*. *Standard Edition*, 23.
—— (1940e [1938]) 'Splitting of the ego in the process of defence'. *Standard Edition*, 23.

—— (1950c [1895]) 'A project for a scientific psychology'. *Standard Edition*, 1.

Green, A. (1983) *Narcissisme de vie, narcissisme de mort*. Paris: Editions de Minuit.

—— (1984) 'Le langage dans la psychanalyse'. *Langages*. Paris: Les Belles-Lettres.

—— (1986) *On Private Madness*. London: Hogarth Press.

—— (1990) *La folie privée*. Paris: Gallimard.

Grunberger, B. (1979) *Narcissism: Psychoanalytic Essays*. New York: International Universities Press.

Hartmann, H. (1964) 'Comments on the psychoanalytic theory of the ego'. In: *Essays on Ego Psychology*. New York: International Universities Press.

Hartocollis, P. (ed.) (1977) *Borderline Personality Disorders*. New York: International Universities Press.

Jacobson, E. (1964) *The Self and the Object World*. New York: International Universities Press.

Kernberg, O. (1967) 'Borderline personality organization'. *Journal of the American Psychoanalytic Association*, 15: 641–685.

—— (1968) 'The treatment of patients with borderline personality organization'. *International Journal of Psycho-Analysis*, 49: 600–619.

—— (1975) *Borderline Conditions and Pathological Narcissism*. New York: Jason Aronson. French translation published by Privat in two volumes entitled *Les troubles limites de la personnalité* (1979) and *La personnalité narcissique* (1988).

Keinberg, O., Selzer, M.A., Koenigsberg, H.W., Carr, A.C. and Appelbaum, A.H. (1989) *Psychodynamic Psychotherapy of Borderline Patients*. New York: Basic Books.

Klein, M. (1946) 'Notes on some schizoid mechanisms'. *International Journal of Psycho-Analysis*, 27: 99–110.

Kohut, H. (1966) 'Forms and transformations of narcissism'. *Journal of the American Psychoanalytic Association*, 14: 243–272.

—— (1971) *The Analysis of the Self*. New York: International Universities Press.

Mahler, M. (1968) *On Human Symbiosis and the Vicissitudes of Individuation*. New York: International Universities Press.

—— , Pine, F. and Bergman, A. (1975) *The Psychological Birth of the Human Infant*. New York: Basic Books.

Pasche, F. (1969) *A partir de Freud*. Paris: Payot.

Potamianou, A. (1980) 'Réflexions psychanalytiques sur la "Prométhia" d'Eschyle', in: *Psychanalyse et Culture grecque*. Paris: Les Belles-Lettres.

—— (1984) *Les enfants de la folie. Violence dans les identifications*. Toulouse: Privat.

—— (1988) 'Figurations du Nirvâna et réaction thérapeutique négative'. *Revue française de Psychanalyse*, 4: 917–935.

—— (1990) 'Réflexions et hypothèses sur la problématique des états limites'. In: *La Psychanalyse: Questions pour demain, Monographies*. Paris: PUF.

Rosenberg, B. (1982) *Masochisme mortifère et masochisme gardien de la vie*. Cahiers du Centre de Psychanalyse, 5: 41–96; and Paris: PUF, 1991.

Rosenfeld, H. (1964) 'On the psychopathology of narcissism'. *International Journal of Psycho-Analysis*, 45: 332–337.

—— (1965) *Psychotic States. A Psychoanalytic Approach*. New York: International Universities Press.

—— (1987) *Impasse and Interpretation*. London and New York: Tavistock Publications.

Winnicott, D. (1958) *Through Paediatrics to Psychoanalysis*. London: Tavistock Publications.

—— (1971), *Playing and Reality*. London: Penguin Books.

Index

117